Praise for *Licensed to Lie*
by Sidney Powell

"*Licensed to Lie* reads like a cross between investigative journalism and courtroom drama. The takeaway is that both Bushies and Obamaites should be very afraid: over the last few years, a coterie of vicious and unethical prosecutors who are unfit to practice law has been harbored within and enabled by the now ironically named Department of Justice."

—WILLIAM HODES, Professor of Law Emeritus,
Indiana University, and coauthor of *The Law of Lawyering*

"When you've finished reading this fast-paced thriller, you will want to stand up and applaud Powell's courage in daring to shine light into the darkest recesses of America's justice system. The only ax Powell grinds here is Truth."

—Patricia Falvey, author of *The Yellow House* and
The Linen Queen, and former managing director
of PricewaterhouseCoopers, LLP

"Last year four government officials demonstrably lied under oath, and nothing has been done to them—two IRS officials, the Attorney General, and James Clapper—which caused Ed Snowden to release the fact that the U.S. is spying on its citizens in violation of the Fourth Amendment. That our government is corrupt is the only conclusion. This book helps the people understand the nature of this corruption—and how it is possible for federal prosecutors to indict and convict the innocent rather than the guilty."

—Victor Sperandeo, CEO, and author of
Trader Vic: Methods of a Wall Street Master

"This book is a testament to the human will to struggle against overwhelming odds to right a wrong and a cautionary tale to all—that true justice doesn't just exist as an abstraction apart from us. True justice is us, making it real through our own actions and our own vigilance against the powerful who cavalierly threaten to take it away."

—MICHAEL ADAMS, PhD, University Distinguished Teaching Associate Professor of English, and Associate Director of the James A. Michener Center for Writers, University of Texas at Austin

"I have covered hundreds of court cases over the years and have witnessed far too often the kind of duplicity and governmental heavy-handedness Ms. Powell describes in her well-written book, *Licensed to Lie.*"

—HUGH AYNESWORTH, journalist, historian, four-time Pulitzer Prize finalist, and author of *November 22, 1963: Witness to History*

Praise for *Three Felonies a Day*
by Harvey A. Silverglate

"Now comes veteran defense lawyer and civil libertarian Harvey A. Silverglate with riveting case studies exposing in technicolor a pattern of serious abuses and convictions of innocent people in some of the most famous (as well as obscure) federal cases of recent decades. Abetted by compliant courts and easily gulled media, the feds brand as criminals good people who intended no crime."
—STUART TAYLOR, JR., *National Journal* columnist
and *Newsweek* contributing editor

"In *Three Felonies a Day*, Harvey A. Silverglate has written a work peerless in revelations about the mad expansion of federal statutes whose result is to define, as criminal, practices no rational citizen could have viewed as illegal. The book is chilling in its detail of the investigations and ruin that have befallen people ground up in this prosecution mill. Whether in the book's scathing chronicle of the destruction of Arthur Andersen, largest accounting firm in the nation, an obscure attorney, or the bizarre government case mounted against a Boston politician—to name a few—Harvey A. Silverglate brings home, unforgettably, the truth that everyone is vulnerable to the terrors wrought by out-of-control prosecutors.

No one reading this can fail to be gripped by these cases, by the hard bright light he shines on every step of these prosecutions, and the mindset that created them. It's a bombshell that was worth waiting for."
—DOROTHY RABINOWITZ, *Wall Street Journal*
editorialist and winner of the Pulitzer Prize

"Gilbert & Sullivan wrote about how the punishment fits the crime. *Three Felonies a Day* shows how federal prosecutors have conceived of something truly frightening—punishment without crime. Harvey A. Silverglate, one of the truly hard-working and uncompromising defenders of our civil liberties, has written the ultimate horror story of prosecutorial abuse. We, the public, should pay attention.

—ERROL MORRIS, documentary filmmaker, winner of the Academy Award for *The Fog of War*, and producer and director of the legendary documentary *The Thin Blue Line*

"This brilliant book lays out the terrifying threat to human rights posed by vindictive federal prosecutions, often sold as moralistic crusades to a gullible press and public. Anyone who cares about American democracy should read this gripping and vitally important exposé."

—STEVEN PINKER, Johnstone Family Professor, Harvard University, and author of *The Stuff of Thought*

"Harvey A. Silverglate masterfully chronicles federal prosecutors' vindictive enlistment of opaque criminal prohibitions to snare the unwary and to stunt civil society. A bloated criminal code that fails to warn before it strikes is tyranny's first cousin."

—BRUCE FEIN, former Associate Deputy Attorney General under President Reagan, and Chairman of the American Freedom Agenda

"*Three Felonies a Day* is one of the most important books to be written about law in a generation. It should be read by anyone who cares about the rule of law.... Law-abiding citizens beware: prosecutors wield Godlike power as they decide how to interpret vague and open-ended statutes that can turn the stuff of everyday life into a federal case. Individual freedom and the rule of law hang in the balance. *Three Felonies a Day* is more than a brilliant collection of great stories about law, although it is sure that: it is a manifesto from one of America's staunchest defenders of civil

liberties demanding that all of us join in the fight for true freedom and the rule of law."
—SUSAN R. ESTRICH, Robert Kingsley Professor of Law
and Political Science, University of Southern California

"In *Three Felonies a Day*, Harvey A. Silverglate zeroes in on governmental misconduct—the brazen abuse by certain federal prosecutors of immense government power for purposes other than justice. The book is a clarion call—to prosecutors, reminding them what their true role is in a democracy—and to the public, reminding everyone of our collective responsibility firmly to oppose, discipline and prohibit such unacceptable abuses in order to protect the Constitution and the rights it guarantees. The book is a compelling read."
—MICHAEL S. GRECO, former President
of the American Bar Association

"To many readers, the book will read like a highlight reel of the most prominent and challenging cases to be brought in recent years.... Silverglate deftly combines the legal sophistication of a criminal defense expert with the plain speech and driving narrative of a journalist."
—MATTHEW W. HUTCHINS, *The Harvard Law Record*

CONVICTION MACHINE

CONVICTION MACHINE

MACHINE

STANDING UP TO FEDERAL PROSECUTORIAL ABUSE

SIDNEY POWELL AND
HARVEY A. SILVERGLATE

Encounter BOOKS

New York • London

First American edition published in 2020 by Encounter Books,
an activity of Encounter for Culture and Education, Inc.,
a nonprofit, tax exempt corporation.
Encounter Books website address: www.encounterbooks.com

Manufactured in the United States and printed on
acid-free paper. The paper used in this publication meets
the minimum requirements of ANSI/NISO Z39.48-1992
(R 1997) (*Permanence of Paper*).

FIRST AMERICAN EDITION

LIBRARY OF CONGRESS CATALOGING-IN-PUBLICATION DATA

Names: Powell, Sidney K., 1955– author. |
Silverglate, Harvey A., 1942– author.
Title: Conviction machine : standing up to federal prosecutorial abuse /
Sidney Powell, Harvey A. Silverglate.
Description: New York : Encounter Books, 2020. |
Includes bibliographical references and index. |
Identifiers: LCCN 2019025112 (print) | LCCN 2019025113 (ebook) |
ISBN 9781594038037 (hardcover) | ISBN 9781594038044 (ebook)
Subjects: LCSH: Prosecution—United States. | Public prosecutors—United
States. | Criminal justice, Administration of—United States.
Classification: LCC KF9640 .P69 2020 (print) | LCC KF9640 (ebook) |
DDC 345.73/01262—dc23
LC record available at https://lccn.loc.gov/2019025112
LC ebook record available at https://lccn.loc.gov/2019025113

CONTENTS

PREFACE

Appalled by the terrible injustices she had recently witnessed in our federal courts, Sidney Powell, a former federal prosecutor, published *Licensed to Lie: Exposing Corruption in the Department of Justice* in 2014.[1] Powell did not want to write *Licensed to Lie*. She was compelled to do so. The book reads like a legal thriller, but sadly it's true, and it names the very powerful people who promoted their own interests by abusing their powers as federal prosecutors. They made up criminal charges, hid evidence, and lied to judges to win convictions. In the process, they destroyed companies, jobs, families, careers, and lives, contributing to an erosion of Americans' faith in our criminal justice system, while simultaneously propelling themselves to positions of great power and prestige in the government and in private practice.

Americans have recently witnessed the perhaps unprecedented abuse of our federal law enforcement agencies, especially the FBI and the Department of Justice, to target the opposition political candidate, morphing into an effort to cripple President Donald Trump upon his unexpected election in 2016. In the process, the FBI and the special counsel, Robert Mueller, targeted not only the president but his closest associates and advisors, looking for anything that might be "pinned" on them. But the long-awaited Mueller Report found no "collusion" between Russia and anyone in the Trump campaign, and it did not recommend prosecution for obstruction of justice. Evidence is coming to light by the day revealing that the entire "Russian collusion" and obstruction narratives were a concoction of the political opposition and high-ranking officials in what used to be our most trusted (at least by many) law enforcement institutions. However, abuse of prosecutorial power is hardly a partisan phenomenon. It is systemic.

Eighty years ago, Attorney General Robert H. Jackson warned against this very abuse of power. He spoke to all the United States attorneys assembled before him in the great hall of the Department of Justice. In 1940 the world was in turmoil. It was a dark time, but his words are still inspiring to those of us who believe in the rule of law.

> The prosecutor has more control over life, liberty, and reputation than any other person in America. His discretion is tremendous.
>
> He can have citizens investigated and, if he is that kind of person, he can have this done to the tune of public statements and veiled or unveiled intimations. Or the prosecutor may choose a more subtle course and simply have a citizen's friends interviewed. The prosecutor can order arrests, present cases to the grand jury in secret session, and on the basis of his one-sided presentation of the facts, can cause the citizen to be indicted and held for trial.
>
> He may dismiss the case before trial, in which case the defense never has a chance to be heard. Or he may go on with a public trial. If he obtains a conviction, the prosecutor can still make recommendations as to sentence, as to whether the prisoner should get probation or a suspended sentence, and after he is put away, as to whether he is a fit subject for parole.
>
> While the prosecutor at his best is one of the most beneficent forces in our society, when he acts from malice or other base motives, he is one of the worst.
>
> These powers have been granted to our law-enforcement agencies because it seems necessary that such a power to prosecute be lodged somewhere. This authority has been granted by people who really wanted the right thing done—wanted crime eliminated—but also wanted the best in our American traditions preserved.

Because of this immense power to strike at citizens, not with mere individual strength, but with all the force of government itself, the post of Federal District Attorney from the very beginning has been safeguarded by presidential appointment, requiring confirmation of the Senate of the United States. You are thus required to win an expression of confidence in your character by both the legislative and the executive branches of the government before assuming the responsibilities of a federal prosecutor.

◆ ◆ ◆

Nothing better can come out of this meeting of law enforcement officers than a rededication to the spirit of fair play and decency that should animate the federal prosecutor. Your positions are of such independence and importance that while you are being diligent, strict, and vigorous in law enforcement you can also afford to be just.

Although the government technically loses its case, it has really won if justice has been done.

◆ ◆ ◆

If the prosecutor is obliged to choose his cases, it follows that he can choose his defendants.

Therein is the most dangerous power of the prosecutor: that he will pick people that he thinks he should get, rather than pick cases that need to be prosecuted. With the law books filled with a great assortment of crimes, a prosecutor stands a fair chance of finding at least a technical violation of some act on the part of almost anyone.

In such a case, it is not a question of discovering the commission of a crime and then looking for the man who has committed it, it is a question of picking the man and then searching the law books, or putting investigators to work, to pin some offense on him. It is in this realm—in which the prosecutor picks some person whom he dislikes or desires to embarrass, or selects some group of unpopular persons and then looks for an offense, that the greatest danger of abuse of prosecuting power lies.[2]

The ability of prosecutors to "pin some offense" on anyone they choose is the subject of Harvey Silverglate's book *Three Felonies a Day: How the Feds Target the Innocent* (2009/2011).[3] As Silverglate demonstrated, the average busy professional going about his business will unknowingly commit three felonies in a normal day because there are so many criminal laws in the code. Through statutory analysis, case law, and the experiences of criminal lawyers defending cases across the spectrum of federal statutes, he showed how federal agents and prosecutors are able to prosecute virtually any person and any undertaking or transaction on felony charges. The feds need only to target somebody who has become an object of prosecutorial interest for any reason whatsoever: The target may be wanted as a witness against a "bigger" target, or the prosecutor may decide that landing a big fish would be good for his or her career, or the target might operate within an area designated as a "priority" area of prosecutorial interest in that district.

Because it is so easy under the broad and vague federal criminal code to turn even facially ordinary daily activity into a prosecutable offense, and because slipshod ethical codes allow prosecutors to get witnesses to "sing and compose," as Professor Alan Dershowitz has felicitously put it, there is never a slow season for federal prosecutions. And the revolving door, leading from high-profile prosecutions to lucrative partnerships in "white shoe" law firms or high positions in government, gives prosecutors all the incentive they need to go after "high-value" targets.

Today, the federal criminal justice system is dangerously effective at turning citizens into convicts. More than twenty million Americans have criminal convictions, while nearly one-third of Americans have a criminal record.[4] More than 3 percent of the American population has served time in prison.[5] The longer one stays in prison, the more difficult it becomes to succeed upon re-entry into the outside world. Everyone and everything outside the prison walls has been changing, while everything inside remains the same: a monotonous and controlled routine in an atmosphere of near-total sensory deprivation. Bernard Kerik, a longtime law enforcement professional who got ensnared in the feds' web, wrote that being in prison is like "dying with your eyes open."[6]

Sidney Powell's client in the Enron Nigerian Barge case, a former Merrill Lynch executive from New York, spent a year in prison. He came out thirty pounds lighter than he went in. Powell will never forget the day she went to the courthouse to secure his release. The United States Court of Appeals for the Fifth Circuit had ordered that he be released "*instanter*." Powell flew to New Jersey for a brief hearing—on an order the likes of which the district judge had never seen. The United States marshals brought the prisoner into court in his orange jumpsuit and chains (they would not let him put on the suit that counsel had brought for him). The hearing was over in less than fifteen minutes, but it took another two hours for the marshals to "process him out." The full story is a nightmare told in *Licensed to Lie.* The client had suffered so much sensory deprivation during his year in prison that when lawyer and client stopped at a hamburger shop, the freed man couldn't walk across the parking lot. He stayed in the back of the car just trying to absorb being in the world again.

Every week or so, the Innocence Project frees someone, usually from a state prison, who has served decades behind bars for a crime that DNA evidence now proves he did not commit. The stories are legion.[7] These people were innocent: They were robbed of their best years because of faulty eyewitness testimony, flawed or dishonest forensics, or prosecutorial misconduct, and they suffered the scorn of society because of a lie. One day in prison is too many for an innocent person. There is no remedy, no amount of money—nothing—that can make up for an innocent person's time in prison. The National Registry of Exonerations now has almost two thousand names. These are people who have been unequivocally exonerated from the crimes for which they were imprisoned. If we are going to have a death penalty, we must be certain the person actually committed the crime. We shudder to think that we have executed people who were innocent, which we undoubtedly have. We must do better.

In our previous books, we wrote about injustices inflicted by the government's well-oiled conviction machine, which serves the ever-burgeoning prison industry but not the citizens of the United States. For example, remember Ted Stevens? The longest-serving Republican in the United States Senate, he was prosecuted by lawyers from the ironically named Public Integrity Section of the Department of Justice along with two assistant United States attorneys from Alaska. Well into the trial, evidence of very serious prosecutorial misconduct began to surface, but it did not get the traction it should have. A jury found Stevens guilty of misstating gifts on his Senate ethics forms.[8] But after Stevens narrowly lost his reelection bid, a young FBI agent filed a "whistleblower complaint" detailing egregious misconduct by the prosecutors and agents.[9] The Department of Justice managed to conceal the complaint from the defense team for Senator Stevens until after the deadline for post-conviction motions had expired.

When the judge overseeing the case, Emmet G. Sullivan, learned of the prosecution's conduct, he blew a fuse. He held the prosecution team in contempt of court, which triggered a requirement within the Justice Department that it appoint a new prosecution team. It took the new team only a few weeks to uncover evidence that the original team had suppressed—evidence that proved the validity of Senator Stevens's defense. Powell is now in the middle of similar litigation involving President Trump's former national security advisor, Michael T. Flynn, who was bludgeoned into a guilty plea by the conviction machine while evidence of his innocence, setup, and wrongful prosecution was withheld.

The problems are beyond dispute. Much ink has been spilled on the ills of the federal criminal justice system, and indeed we each have separately written a book about injustices done by the conviction machine. As we have traveled across the country speaking on the subjects raised by our books, we are always asked the same question: "OK, you've outlined the problems. Now, what can we do about it?"

We write to suggest ways to stop the gears of the conviction machine from grinding our constitutional rights and the rule of law to dust—destroying the lives of too many of our fellow citizens in the process. This book proposes realistic solutions, gleaned from our experiences as a former federal prosecutor and as defense counsel. Some of these ideas are simple and uncontroversial. Some are legislative fixes, some need to be undertaken by the judiciary, others require action by the executive branch—but together the policies proposed herein aim to make our justice system less corrupt and more just.

CHAPTER ONE

CATCH 22

What Talking to the FBI Can Do to You

The government has a lethal weapon it can deploy at will against any unwary citizen. It is the deadly combination of the ability of federal agents to interview people without counsel; to formalize that interview in their own terms, language, and sequence; and then to seek prosecution of that person for the felony of making a false statement to a federal government official, under Title 18, United States Code, section 1001. False-statement cases normally arise incidentally when government agents are investigating a matter and the interviewee makes a misstatement about that matter. Agents then seek to get to the truth by giving 1001 warnings to coax truthful information from the suspect. But the government has become much more aggressive about abusing the process to create stand-alone offenses and add-on charges to force guilty pleas.

In federal investigations, the FBI's standard practice is for two agents to interview a witness anywhere, at any time, and usually by surprise. One agent usually takes notes while the other questions the witness, and then, based on the written notes, the agents write a summary report of the interview on a numbered government form called a 302. Despite the modern ease of digital audio and video recording capabilities on every cell phone, the FBI deliberately does not record interviews. As one might imagine, this allows the agents extraordinary leeway and untrammeled discretion in the way they write their 302 reports. Judges rarely permit defense counsel to see the agents' original notes, even though there are often material differences between those notes and the 302. Add the federal statute embodied in 18 U.S.C. § 1001, under which it is a felony to make a false statement to a government agent, and the prosecution has an industrial-size grinder for its conviction machine—and under its total control.

The most glaring recent example of this abuse was described by James Comey, the former FBI director, when he bragged about how he had circumvented White House protocols and sent two agents to ambush-interview Lieutenant General Michael Flynn, the national security advisor to President Donald Trump, just days into the new administration. The FBI deputy director, Andrew McCabe, had set up Flynn for the interview by suggesting it was a training exercise in which, of course, he would cooperate with the FBI, and according to McCabe, suggested to Flynn that counsel need not be involved. The FBI already had recordings and transcripts of Flynn's conversations with the Russian ambassador to the United States, which is what the agents were asking him about, and there was nothing wrong with his having the conversations. In fact, it was Flynn's job to do so. The sole purpose of the visit was to put General Flynn in a perjury trap.[†]

Rod Blagojevich, former governor of Illinois, learned a thing or two about how the feds operate when they want a conviction,

---

† The calls with the Russian ambassador were among hundreds of calls Flynn had participated in since Donald Trump was elected. He knew the FBI agents had recordings and transcripts of his conversations. He shared his best recollection with the agents, who left with the firm conviction that he had been honest with them. In documents the Office of Special Counsel hid until after Flynn pleaded guilty, the FBI and the DOJ had cleared him of any wrongdoing. On the eve of Flynn's leaving the White House, the FBI made material changes in the 302. In fact, McCabe's personal special counsel Lisa Page made edits to the 302. Then her paramour Peter Strzok added "substantive statements" that appeared nowhere in the notes of the agents. By the

especially when it comes to a high-profile target like a sitting governor. He made the mistake of talking to the FBI agents who asked
to speak to him.

Patrick Fitzgerald, the United States attorney in Chicago back
when Blagojevich was arrested in 2008, likewise knew how the DOJ
assures itself of getting its man. Blagojevich's initial charge sheet
consisted of a plethora of spectacular-sounding and media-grab-
bing corruption allegations. However, the later-issued formal indictment contained, in addition, two rather ordinary-sounding
counts accusing the governor of lying, twice, during a March 2005
FBI interview.

The feds alleged that the governor tried to mislead federal
agents when he claimed, in his early interview, that he maintained
a "firewall" between his politics and his work as governor. Further,
charged the feds, Blagojevich lied when he claimed that he "does
not track, or want to know, who contributes to him or how much
they are contributing to him." Fitzgerald and his fellow prosecutors charged that both assertions were untrue and violated the
false-statements statute.[1]

The jury convicted Blagojevich of lying to the FBI but dead-
locked on all the corruption-related offenses (setting the stage for
a retrial in which the governor was convicted of corruption). Addressing the public from the courthouse steps after his first trial,
Blagojevich reiterated that he'd told the truth. He added a detail
that drew little attention from the news media that seemed so im-
pressed, even giddy, with the prosecutors' success in convicting a
governor. Blagojevich revealed that the FBI agents had refused his
request that a stenographer or other means of verbatim recordation

time they made these changes, it was three weeks after their ambush-interview of Flynn. They
subsequently reentered the "final 302" in the FBI's Sentinel system for use by the special counsel
in May 2017. Robert Mueller later indicted Flynn for making false statements to the agents in
violation of 18 U.S.C. § 1001, even though Comey and McCabe admitted in prior congressional
testimony that the agents who interviewed Flynn believed he was being truthful in his answers.
Although Judge Emmet G. Sullivan ordered the special counsel to produce all material relevant to
the initial interview of Flynn, key documents—including the agents' original interview notes and
original Form 302—are still missing. The Flynn case is discussed at greater length in Chapter 5.

be present when they interviewed him, before indicting him for false statements.

Sheldon Sorosky, one of the trial lawyers for Blagojevich, shed further light on what happened regarding the "false statements" charges. Sorosky pointed out when Harvey Silverglate spoke to him by phone that there were actually *two* FBI interviews, but the governor was charged with lying at only the first of them. Before the first interview, Blagojevich and his counsel asked that the Q&A be recorded verbatim. In accordance with bureau policy, the government refused the request. Rather than walk out of the room, Blagojevich and his lawyers, obviously aware of the atmospherics (and press leaks) that would result if a sitting governor refused to answer the FBI's questions, agreed to sit for the nonrecorded interview.

After that first interview, the agents asked for a follow-up session. This time, Blagojevich and his lawyer insisted that a certified stenographer be present to make a verbatim record. The bureau, obviously eager to conduct the follow-up, made an exception to its normal nonrecording rule, and the second interview was stenographically recorded.

Four years later the government indicted Blagojevich for, among other things, allegedly lying about maintaining a separation between fundraising activities and his official gubernatorial duties. Sorosky, who was present at the first interview, told Silverglate that he had no memory of his client ever making such an assertion to the agents, and assured him that nobody on Blagojevich's side who was present at the interview had either a memory or notes of the governor's making such a statement. Yet when Blagojevich was indicted for the alleged lie, the government claimed that the statement had indeed been made, and presumably government agents at the Q&A were prepared so to testify.

Revealingly, *no* false-statement charges emanated from the *second* interview, at which the governor and his lawyers had insisted that a stenographer be present as a condition for agreeing to the interview. After the "false statements" conviction, Silverglate wrote a column for *Forbes* posing an intriguing question: "If the first interview had a verbatim transcript, would prosecutors still have had the 'false statement' charge at their disposal?"[2]

Blagojevich decided in the middle of his trial not to testify, which obviously made it difficult for jurors to question the veracity of the FBI agents' account of what occurred at the first interview session—especially without a tape recording or stenographic transcript to rebut the FBI's version. But even if the governor had gone forward with his initial plan to testify, it would have been his word against that of the agents. It would have been an allegedly corrupt politician's word against that of upstanding officials working for the venerable Department of Justice and the storied FBI. Very few defendants win such a credibility contest.

Blagojevich's fate on the false-statement charge was sealed by the routine FBI practice of prohibiting verbatim recording of interviews. The FBI and the DOJ made sure he would be convicted of two felonies for which he could receive as much as five years on each count.

• • •

With the advent of ubiquitous digital recording capabilities and the growing revelations of abuses by the FBI and the DOJ, the practice of not recording interviews has come under increasing scrutiny—as well it should.[3]

On May 22, 2014, the Department of Justice released an internal memo purportedly heralding change. The memo, "Policy Concerning Electronic Recording of Statements," drew courted praise from the media. But closer examination shows that it changed little. The policy "establishes a presumption" that federal investigators "will electronically record statements made by individuals in their custody." Remarkably, however, the majority of FBI interviews are with witnesses or suspects before an arrest has been made, and so they are not "in custody." Moreover, a "presumption" of recording is hardly a requirement, and as the memo is only for internal "guidance," it is toothless. Indeed, the exceptions to this policy swallow the rule.[4]

Despite this small change, the FBI retains a dangerous power it has had for decades: to trap and then prosecute—or threaten to prosecute—anyone in the bureau's or a federal prosecutor's sights. Anyone who speaks with a federal agent is a potential candidate for a false-statement prosecution.

How does this work? And why has the FBI resisted a universal *requirement* that interviews routinely be recorded except perhaps in the most extraordinary situations?

The answer begins with the so-called "false-statements statute," section 1001 of the federal criminal code.[†] It has long been a felony, punishable by up to five years in prison, for anyone who agrees to speak with a member of the executive branch of the federal government—including but not limited to FBI and other investigative agents—to make a false material statement. Materiality is judged, not surprisingly, by the relevance of a statement to a matter in which the feds have some role or interest, and over which there is federal jurisdiction.

What this means, in theory, is that anytime an agent comes calling on a potential witness, that witness has two choices: either decline to speak altogether, or else tell the truth, the whole truth, and nothing but the truth—with no omissions of anything the FBI might later decide it wanted to hear the witness say. In a surprising number of instances, witnesses approached by federal agents choose to answer questions rather than shut up or at least place a phone call to a lawyer for advice. And in a surprising number of these cases, even a truthful answer to a question can result in the threat of a false-statement charge.

Indeed, one of the most common counts to appear in a federal indictment is a charge under the false-statement statute. In a rather

---

† 18 U.S.C. § 1001 provides, in pertinent part, that "whoever, in any matter within the jurisdiction [of the federal government] knowingly and willfully...makes any materially false...statement" is guilty of a felony punishable by five years in prison.

large number of cases—we suspect it's a majority—where a defendant spoke with prosecutors or agents, and where the interview or discussion was not recorded verbatim, there is a false-statement charge. This is what criminal defense lawyers call a "make-weight" or "backup" charge: even if the defendant is acquitted of the underlying criminal charge (e.g., securities fraud, money laundering, sale of narcotics), he is likely to be convicted of making a false statement. This vulnerability to conviction under the false-statement statute results when a target's claim of what he did or did not say (unrecorded!) to the agent differs from the agent's claimed recollection embodied in the FBI 302 report of the interview. Many a defendant, found innocent of any underlying crime, has found himself hooked for a false statement.

Just ask George Papadopoulos or others investigated by Robert Mueller, the special counsel, who have been compelled by the sheer weight and cost of defending against federal criminal charges to plead guilty to false-statement charges stemming from their FBI interviews. General Flynn's case is especially egregious because both James Comey, the former FBI director, and Andrew McCabe, the assistant director, testified to Congress that the FBI agents who ambush-interviewed Flynn believed he was telling the truth.[5] He was forced to plead guilty because of financial and psychological exhaustion from the entire ordeal—exacerbated by threats to indict his son, who had merely handled administrative tasks for their fledgling company.[6]

This still understates the true perniciousness of the false-statement statute. It places the interviewee at the complete mercy of the interviewing agents. It readily ensnares anyone who accedes to an agent's request for an interview. The false-statement statute and the nonrecording rule comprise "the perfect cocktail for manipulating witnesses and in effect composing their testimony."[7]

When federal agents approach a witness, they request an interview right then and there. The approach is usually an ambush: completely unexpected and at the witness's home, or at work, or on the street—anywhere. If the interview is noncustodial, as in Flynn's case, the agents do not even have to warn the person with whom they are speaking that their statements can be used against them and any false statement is a felony. In fact, in Flynn's case, a group of the highest echelon of the FBI had an extensive strategy meeting on how to approach Flynn and interview him without alerting him that they were targeting him. They wanted to keep him "relaxed" and "unguarded." It worked. The agents reported back that they visited with him alone, he was "unguarded," and he clearly saw them as "allies."

If the witness dares request that the encounter be recorded, by either the agent or the witness, the agent advises it is against FBI policy to record such interviews. The FBI is sufficiently serious about adherence to this rule that an agent will refrain from conducting an interview altogether rather than record it or allow it to be recorded by the interviewee or his lawyer.[†] This must change—immediately. It simply encourages abuses and wrongful prosecutions.

After an interview, the agents create the Form 302 report. This self-selected rendition becomes the government's official version of what was asked and answered during the interview. If the government is interested in having the interviewee become a witness against the target of the investigation, an agent or prosecutor approaches him and suggests that the witness be prepared to repeat the story—under oath—to a grand jury that would then issue an indictment against the target. A witness may not refuse to testify to a grand jury unless some recognized legal privilege intervenes. The agent or prosecutor usually reminds the witness of what he supposedly said during the FBI interview.

---

† Harvey Silverglate has had many situations in his own law practice in which an agent has requested to interview a client. In one situation of which he has a particularly vivid memory, he produced the client at his law office in Boston; two agents arrived and introduced themselves. When he placed his audiocassette recording device visibly on the table, the agents asked that it be removed, stating that they were not allowed to record interviews except via handwritten notes. Silverglate offered a copy of the recording to the agents while still refusing to remove the device, whereupon the agents rose and left, with the interview never conducted.

When an interviewee disagrees with the FBI's version of what he said, the agent, or a federal prosecutor, reminds the witness that it is the witness's word against that of two FBI agents and their official Form 302 report, and it is a crime to lie to an agent just as it is a crime for a witness to tell a false story to a grand jury or at a trial.[†] (So unless the witness is prepared to adopt what the 302 report *says* that he previously told the agents, he is caught between a rock and a hard place—between a charge that he lied when speaking to the agents or that he committed perjury before the grand jury or in court.) This practice effectively forces the witness to succumb to the strong suggestions of the agents or prosecutors that he adopt whatever the 302 report says he told the agents. A prosecutor can readily make such a suggestion to the witness, since the prosecutor rarely questions his FBI agents. This entire practice provides too great an opportunity for mistake and mischief by even the most scrupulous agents.

•   •   •

Remarkably, the FBI has no intention of abandoning its selective and advantageous nonrecording rule, and Congress has shown no interest in changing the way the game is played. Robert Mueller, as the FBI director, testified in 2007 that the rule was a salutary one with a genuine law enforcement purpose.[8] By that time, however, it was obvious that recording devices were becoming cheap and ubiquitous, so Mueller omitted the claimed unavailability of recording devices as a reason for maintaining the rule.

Mueller rejected the view of some United States attorneys that confessions would be more believable had they been recorded, but he said the FBI had given "additional guidance to our Special Agents in Charge, liberalizing the incidents of where" the bureau would agree to recording.

---

† Lying under oath before a grand jury or a trial jury is the crime of perjury, likewise punishable by up to five years in prison. See 18 U.S.C. § 1623.

Even though Mueller could no longer credibly contend that recording devices were scarce, expensive, or bulky to carry, he claimed a budgetary objection to a rule requiring routine recording of *suspects'* statements. He did not even touch on the notion of recording statements of mere witnesses. According to Mueller, the prospect of transcribing interviews and determining how they all would be handled was more than the bureau could manage. If that is true, the bureau should be shuttered for good.

Unfortunately, Congress retreated to its typical deference to the FBI.† In his 2007 testimony, Mueller prevailed without having to address the real reason the FBI preferred to maintain the antitaping regulation: It allowed the federal conviction machine to roll on.

The Supreme Court, especially Justice Ruth Bader Ginsburg, has caught on to the government's abuses of the false-statement statute, but hasn't put a stop to it. In *Brogan v. United States*,[9] the Court addressed the situation created by a suspect who merely says "no" when asked a loaded question that implies his guilt, such as: "When did you last beat your wife?" Agents are not, of course, easily fooled by this so-called "exculpatory no" response to an obviously loaded, incriminating question. Several courts of appeal had ruled that an "exculpatory no" could not be deemed a false statement under section 1001. But the Supreme Court reversed those courts, holding that the statute had to be taken literally since its text contains no exception for "the mere denial of wrongdoing."

This literal reading of the statute did not sit well with several of the justices. Justice David Souter, while going along with the outcome of the case, urged in a concurring opinion that Congress consider remedying "the risks inherent in the statute's current breadth." He agreed with Justice Ginsburg, who, while concurring in the majority, also issued an extraordinary condemnation of the pernicious effect of the statute as written and as used, and abused, by prosecutors.

---

† The FBI's written policy on electronic recordings is included in the Appendices.

Justice Ginsburg's biting concurring opinion focused directly on the real problem posed by the false-statement statute. She noted that it aimed to prevent "proscribed falsehoods designed to elicit a benefit from the Government or to hinder Government operations." But she recognized that government agents were using the statute "to generate felonies."

Justice Ginsburg observed that Brogan had been surprised and trapped in an interview without counsel. Brogan "divulged nothing more" than a simple "no," an "unadorned denial [that] misled no one." She berated the government for what she deemed other "not altogether uncommon episodes" in the same vein. Because the typical interviewee is not usually a suspect, he is not warned of his rights, and he is encouraged to speak rather than to exercise his right to decline the interview. No oath is administered, so the interviewee does not recognize the profound trap into which he can easily fall merely by denying guilt, even with a single unsworn word. It is a technique, complained Justice Ginsburg, for generating a crime even when the underlying crime being investigated may be a state offense instead of a federal one, or when the underlying offense is barred by the statute of limitations. The false-statement statute is, essentially, an insidious trap for the unwary, including the innocent.

"It is doubtful," wrote Justice Ginsburg, that "Congress intended section 1001 to cast so large a net." It was enacted, she noted, in 1863 as a measure against the filing of fraudulent claims with the government during the Civil War. Creative federal agents and prosecutors have broadened its use over the years. Yet, she complained, Congress never amended the statute to cover "suspects' false denials of criminal conduct, in the course of informal interviews initiated by Government agents." She decried how the statute allowed law enforcement to manufacture a crime.

Justices John Paul Stevens and Stephen Breyer went further and formally *dissented* from such a literal interpretation of the false-statement statute. In any event, the Court in *Brogan* did not reach to the heart or extent of the problem posed. The false-statement statute is a powerful weapon for prosecutorial abuse. It allows the government to manipulate entirely innocent interviewees, rendering them helpless tools of the conviction machine—forced to bear false witness against themselves or others.

The solution to the abuse of these practices by the FBI and federal prosecutors when dealing with the section 1001 false-statement statute and the attendant 302 trap rests with Congress, which need only mandate that the FBI record all interviews or provide that 1001 charges cannot be threatened or prosecuted in the absence of a warned and fully recorded statement from which the alleged false statements arise.

•   •   •

The states have already begun these reforms. A rather modest but highly effective reform of police interview practices was ordered by the Supreme Judicial Court (SJC) of Massachusetts in an opinion issued in 2004 in the case of *Commonwealth v. DiGiambattista*.[10]

At the time of *DiGiambattista*, the SJC said that only two states, Alaska and Minnesota, required an instruction that interrogations be recorded, and three states—Illinois, Maine, and Texas—plus the District of Columbia imposed a recording requirement via legislation for certain types of cases and interrogations. Since then, other states have followed suit, with numerous variations on the theme. As of early 2019, the high courts of Alaska, Minnesota, New Jersey, and Arkansas have all ruled that police must record interrogations conducted in the investigation of all crimes, and Utah and Indiana's courts have required such recordings for felony investigations. A further eighteen state legislatures ranging from liberal California to deep red Nebraska have passed laws requiring the recordation of suspect interviews in specified felony cases.[11]

This gradual progress at the state level is the result of hard work done by various reform groups that recognize the danger inherent in unrecorded witness and suspect interviews. The Innocence Project considers the electronic recording of interrogations to be "the single best reform available to stem the tide of false confessions."[12] Similarly, the National Association of Criminal Defense Lawyers describes electronic recording as "the most objective means for evaluating what occurred during an interrogation, what the suspect and law enforcement agents said and did...and the accuracy of any statement."[13]

Given the ubiquity of inexpensive and reliable recording equipment, and the fact that every federal agent carries a cell phone that can record audio or video, Congress should impose a recording requirement for *any* FBI interview. There is simply no valid reason to continue to allow any opportunity for government abuses of the interview process to *create* false-statement crimes. Another option would be for Congress to enact a simple statute that allows the government to introduce at trial and prove a false statement only by statements that have been recorded in full and after warnings.

Nonrecorded interviews, under such a regime, could be used by agents as investigative leads, but would not be admissible evidence in court. This would end an FBI tactic that has probably resulted in more false testimony, and false convictions, than any other single practice in federal law enforcement. Every federal agent currently is equipped with a smartphone capable of recording audio (and, indeed, video). This is a cost-free and immediate solution to an unnecessary, unfair, unjust, and widespread problem that diminishes the credibility of every law enforcement agency that does not use it already.

In the meantime, those seeking truth and fairness in the system of criminal justice, as well as those concerned with self-protection, should be alert to the dangers of agreeing to an interview by the FBI or any other federal official, and should warn others as well.[14] And, it is necessary to remember, this includes any and every federal employee, even one's local postmaster. Never speak to any federal officer unless your attorney is present and the interview is being recorded—period.

CHAPTER TWO

THERE'S NOTHING GRAND ABOUT GRAND JURIES

Except Their Size

Many people have heard the adage: "A prosecutor can get a grand jury to indict a ham sandwich." That proved true most recently when Robert Mueller's handpicked team of legal eagles indicted a Russian company that did not exist.[1] The special counsel also indicted a Russian company on "unprecedented" charges, meaning, in plain speak, the prosecutors made up a crime—again.[2] It happened many times in the Enron case (as described in detail in *Licensed to Lie*). Prosecutors pieced together parts of different statutes to create a new crime on which to indict Arthur Andersen LLP, destroying the company, only to have the Supreme Court reverse the case later. Prosecutors also made up crimes against four Merrill Lynch executives.

Creating crimes is the job of Congress, and because conviction brings with it the "moral condemnation of society," the Supreme Court has said the law must be clear, and give fair notice that the conduct is criminal, before someone may be convicted of violating it.[3] That does not stop creative, overzealous, and sometimes malevolent prosecutors who have learned that they can punch their tickets to fame and fortune by "taking down" high-profile targets. Grand juries have become "rubber-stamps" which merely do the bidding of federal prosecutors.

• • •

The right to presentation of a felony allegation to a grand jury is enshrined in the Fifth Amendment to the United States Constitution. It provides, inter alia:

> No person shall be held to answer for a capital, or otherwise in-famous crime, unless on a presentment or indictment of a grand jury, except in cases arising in the land or naval forces, or in the militia, when in actual service in time of war or public danger;....

Our Founding Fathers envisioned the grand jury serving as a citizen's protection against government overreach.[4] In practice today, the grand jury serves two primary functions: it investigates criminal offenses, issuing subpoenas for documentary evidence and witnesses; and it returns indictments or "no bills" on charges that are presented—in both situations at the direction of and under the control of a federal prosecutor. It is an exceedingly rare occasion when the grand jury serves the purpose the Founders intended: to screen the credible from the noncredible or to impose the limits and standards of the citizens on otherwise unbridled prosecutors. We need to restore that protection.

In addition to its origins in the Fifth Amendment, the modern grand jury is a creature of Rule 6 of the Federal Rules of Criminal Procedure.[5] Grand jurors are usually selected to serve for six to eighteen months at a time, and they sit as a group of sixteen to twenty-three people. Grand juries operate in secrecy, and no defendant or witness may have counsel with him or her in the grand jury room, although one may request to leave the room to consult with counsel, who normally waits impatiently in the courthouse corridor. Other than the defendant or witness, only the prosecutor, grand jurors, stenographer, and bailiff are permitted inside the grand jury room. To call the grand jury intimidating is an understatement.

The "grand" jury is so named because it is much larger than the jury we see on television in the courtroom deciding cases. In criminal cases, those are "petit" juries, usually composed of twelve people; there can be fewer jurors in civil cases.

The role of the grand jury is very different from that of the trial jury. The grand jury listens only to witnesses presented to it by the prosecution, at prosecutors' direction and supervision, and then the grand jury votes—on the recommendation of the prosecution—on whether there is "probable cause" to support the charges presented to it in an indictment drafted by the prosecutor. By choosing what the grand jury hears, any prosecutor can easily lead a grand jury to do whatever he wants—return the indictment as drafted, return a "true bill" on part of it, or return a "no bill" rejecting all the charges.

Probable cause, despite the common meaning of "probable," does not mean "more likely than not" that a crime occurred. Instead, the law defines "probable cause" as whether a reasonable person, considering the "totality of the circumstances," would conclude that there was "a substantial chance of criminal activity."[6]

The Founding Fathers intended the grand jury to be a check and balance to overzealous, overcharging prosecutors. The grand jury can call witnesses, ask questions itself, and, in theory, make its own decisions. As a practical matter, however, the grand jury merely does what the prosecutor wants it to do, and only the prosecutor calls witnesses before a grand jury. She decides whether the person is a subject, a target, or just a witness. Depending on how the witness testifies—and the "zeal" of the prosecutor—that status may change. The prosecutor is thus able to shape a charge, and to get witnesses to play along, behind closed doors.

For example, in the Enron Nigerian Barge case involving a year-end business transaction between Merrill Lynch executives and the Enron energy company, prosecutors subpoenaed Merrill's in-house counsel to testify before the grand jury. When the prosecutor Andrew Weissmann did not like her testimony because it did not fit with his "view" of the case, he ratcheted up her status from "witness" to "subject" of the grand jury investigation, meaning she was that much closer to being indicted herself. Naturally, that made her try harder to appease the prosecutors.

For Powell's client in the case, it was even worse. Imagine a middle-aged executive who has been law-abiding all his life, a managing director for Merrill Lynch responsible for $800 million worth of hard assets that Merrill leased. He was merely doing his job, working long hours, and trying to wrap things up at year's end. Everyone in the firm was trying to get out for Christmas and the New Year's holiday, hoping not to be working in between. A deal came in that no one really liked, but it was for a big and successful client. This managing director especially didn't like it. He told everyone he thought it was a terrible deal and the company should not do it.

He wasn't on the phone call with all the parties when the deal was discussed, but he had reviewed the deal memo and made a long list of all the risks associated with the small $7 million investment that Merrill was considering making. Executives way above his pay grade approved the deal—without listening to him personally, and over the objections he had expressed to everyone to whom he had access, including in-house counsel. All he knew about the conversation discussing the deal was what other people had told him, which is legally defined as hearsay, and in theory not admissible as evidence.

Two years later he found himself subpoenaed to testify in front of a federal grand jury and threatened with indictment. Nonetheless, he appeared there voluntarily, and also testified before the Securities and Exchange Commission. He wanted to cooperate because he believed in our judicial system. He knew the deal at issue was done properly, with counsel guiding it all the way. On top of that, he was the one who had tried to get everyone to drop the deal on its merits, as it held too much risk and too little upside.

Sworn on the Bible to testify to the truth, which he believed every-one would understand, he sat in the grand jury room surrounded by prosecutors, with twenty-three federal grand jurors staring at him. The expensive lawyer that Merrill Lynch hired to represent him was sitting outside in the hall. If he had a question he wanted to ask legal counsel, he would have to request permission to leave the grand jury room. That doesn't look good, and few witnesses do it.

Of course the prosecutor starts out seeming like a nice guy, but soon it turns nasty. He asks about that phone call where the deal was struck, but the witness wasn't on the call. How do you answer that question? The witness's recollection of the deal from two years earlier is vague, and he only knows what other people have told him. He has an "understanding" of it all, but he doesn't know if his understanding is correct. As the witness tries to ex-plain these uncertainties to the prosecutor and the grand jury, the prosecutor says, "I'm instructing you to share your personal understanding of the phone call with the grand jury—whether it is accurate or not."

That seems safe enough. The prosecutor just wants your per-sonal understanding, and it doesn't matter if your understand-ing is wrong. After all, he said "whether it's accurate or not." You shouldn't need to worry about perjury, then. Perjury is a material false statement made with knowledge that it is false.[7] But if your answer doesn't have to be factually correct, then it can't possibly be perjury. Right?

Wrong! The next thing you know, you've been indicted, not only for the business transaction you strongly advised against, but also for perjury and obstruction of justice for testifying wrongly—the grand jury says—about your *personal understanding* of the phone call you were not on, after you were told that your testimony did not even have to be correct. On top of that, you've lost your job of two decades.

This happened. And once an indictment is returned, the world assumes the defendant is guilty. Realistically, the presumption of innocence goes out the window when the judge reads the indictment to the jury at trial. Once indicted, you are a criminal defendant. No one ever looks at someone the same way again.

Even worse, the road from indictment to conviction is direct and all but inevitable, because federal prosecutions have a staggering conviction rate of more than 95 percent—mostly by plea agreements. The deck is stacked in favor of the federal prosecutor. Most people can't face the might and weight of a federal prosecution. Once indicted, they plead guilty, even if they are innocent.[8] Is this justice?

◆ ◆ ◆

In 2000, a Commission to Reform the Federal Grand Jury created by the National Association of Criminal Defense Lawyers proposed meaningful changes, some similar to the ones we propose below.[9] Two decades earlier, the American Bar Association had conducted a review of the grand jury system, but little more was done than holding congressional hearings and deciding to have grand jury proceedings recorded. Those changes had "very little impact on the core concerns that fueled the calls for modest reforms," the commission noted. Meanwhile, "the number of federal prosecutors has exploded while effective controls against federal grand jury abuses have dwindled." Reform was needed more than ever, so that the grand jury "might again function as most feel it should—as an investigative arm of the government capable of combating crime, but also, simultaneously, a critical protector of citizens' rights."[10]

We propose three primary changes that would substantially improve the grand jury process, and none would even require legislation. They would require only a policy change in the Department of Justice. First, expand the training of grand jurors. Second, allow defendant's counsel who wish to do so to present one hour of evidence to the grand jury for every four counts of an indictment, in addition to our recommendation in Chapter 7 that indictments be limited to fewer counts in most cases.[11] Third, we recommend that counsel for any target or subject of a grand jury investigation be allowed to be present in the grand jury room.

As it stands now, grand jurors receive limited instructions and are handed over to prosecutors with whom they quickly bond. More training of grand jurors is needed, and it should not only cover the original purpose of the grand jury to serve as a protection against government overreach and abuses, but also include modern-day examples of cases in which the government has been reversed for creating crimes, hiding exculpatory evidence, and overreaching. The Department of Justice, the American Bar Association, and the National Association of Criminal Defense Lawyers (NACDL) could collaborate to write a handbook that should be required reading for all grand jurors. There are plenty of examples in this book. Perhaps grand jurors should be required to read *Three Felonies a Day* and *Licensed to Lie*. It would require only a day or so more time to provide meaningful additional training for grand jurors, and examples of real-world, recent abuses would bring home the problems.

Counsel for the defense should be given some reasonable amount of time to present evidence to the grand jury when so desired.[12] While we certainly don't discourage requiring the government to present exculpatory evidence to the grand jury, we think the far better antidote to grand jury abuses would be to allow defense counsel, at the defendant's option, to present one hour of evidence to the grand jury for every four counts of the indictment against the defendant. As a practical matter, we doubt many defendants would even do this—and of those that do opt to present evidence in their defense to the grand jury, most would probably not use their full allotted time.

Many defendants in federal cases are guilty of some criminal conduct and are often looking for the best plea deal they can get, as quickly and inexpensively as they can get it. Allowing defense counsel to present evidence to the grand jury would, however, be a significant benefit in those close cases—which often should not be indicted at all—in which prosecutors play games, try to make examples of select people, present novel "theories" of a crime, and overreach the letter and spirit of their most solemn duties.

As a third remedy, we urge that counsel be present whenever a target or a subject is being questioned in front of a grand jury, and of course that the witness be given a *Miranda* warning. Often, a grand jury proceeds without ever questioning the target, but if it does, counsel should be present in the grand jury room solely for the purpose of advising the witness.[13] This eliminates the need for the witness to run outside the room to consult with counsel, could speed up the process, and would certainly help temper the prosecutor's worst excesses.

Otherwise, the grand jury becomes an intimidation game, a perjury trap, and a crushing gear of the conviction machine. We can think of no legitimate reason to prohibit counsel of a subject or target or mere witness from being present for any questioning of his client. The grand jury setting is ripe for far too many shenanigans by prosecutors who have forgotten that their job is to seek justice—not convictions. If the average jury is susceptible to "improper suggestions, insinuations" and the like from prosecutors, who are viewed as representing a power obliged to govern impartially, grand jurors are even more so, because the prosecutor is often alone with them and because they look to the prosecutor for guidance at every turn.[14]

In the decades since the ABA and NACDL studies and recommendations, we have witnessed ever-increasing misconduct and egregious prosecutorial abuses. The corrections proposed here to restore balance to our grand jury system cannot continue to wait. There is no reason for innocent people like Senator Ted Stevens, those at Arthur Andersen LLP, Merrill Lynch executives, and countless others to be indicted on the concocted charges of prosecutors who see the destruction of their victims as blood sport. It is difficult enough for defendants with status and resources; one shudders to think of the grueling experience faced by ordinary people who are unfortunate enough to get caught in the conviction machine.

Each of these changes could be instituted immediately as policy by the Department of Justice, or could be legislatively imposed. We would suggest trying a policy approach first to see what the response is. These simple and easy steps, if adopted, could quickly restore the original meaning and purpose to the role of the grand jury as a check and balance to the otherwise unfettered power of the prosecutor.

CHAPTER THREE

ACTS OF GOD

Discovery and the Hide-and-Seek Problem

Over the past twenty years, gamesmanship has been on the rise in the legal profession. We can't explain why, but more attorneys have lost their moral compass and now practice tactics of destruction instead of professionalism, conflict resolution, or truth-seeking. This is even more apparent among prosecutors, too many of whom are willing to hide evidence favorable to the defense or employ other ethically dubious tactics to win a conviction.

In a criminal case, the simple truth is this: The government holds all the cards. The defense does not know what the defense does not know. But when a person's liberty is at stake, "go fish" is not enough. As the defense team for Michael Flynn wrote in one of its briefs before Judge Emmett G. Sullivan, "playing cat-and-mouse with the Due Process Clause is the opposite of what the *Brady-Bagley-Giglio* line of cases is all about."[1]

In theory, a prosecutor, whether state or federal, is obligated to disclose to defense counsel all exculpatory evidence that might prove useful in demonstrating a defendant to be either innocent or merely less culpable than the criminal charges against him would suggest. This doctrine grew out of an important 1963 United States Supreme Court case, *Brady v. Maryland*,[2] which, although decided with two dissents, has over the years become accepted law in all fifty states and within the federal criminal justice system. The *Brady* court viewed this doctrine as an extension of earlier high court cases that ruled that the knowing use of perjured testimony by prosecutors violated the due process of law guaranteed by the Fourteenth Amendment.[3] In our adversarial criminal justice system, the Supreme Court noted, the law "casts the prosecutor in the role of an architect" of a criminal trial. Such proceedings must not be "the result of guile," and they must be generally fair. To that end, the Court said:

> We now hold that the suppression by the prosecution of evidence favorable to an accused upon request violates due process where the evidence is material either to guilt or to punishment, irrespective of the good faith or bad faith of the prosecution.

The so-called "*Brady* rule," requiring a prosecutor to disclose "exculpatory evidence" to the defense, has undergone various alterations over time at both the state and federal levels. Generally, the Supreme Court and various state courts have refined the rule. The prosecutorial obligation has come to include disclosure, for example, of any evidence that might impeach the credibility of a prosecutorial witness, as well as an affirmative obligation to turn over any evidence that might tend to show the defendant's innocence or even to reduce his degree of blameworthiness. Further, it has come to include exculpatory evidence in the hands of law enforcement officials, even if not in the prosecutor's own file.[4] Thus, prosecutors have been admonished to affirmatively search for and inquire about evidence located in the files of other law enforcement agencies.[5] In the modern criminal justice system, with its increasing use of computerized records, there is no legitimate excuse for failing to consolidate the investigative, enforcement, and prosecutorial files.

Prosecutors must exert control over these agencies to accumulate in the government's file all the materials and information relevant to the investigation.

• • •

Adherence to the *Brady* rule could have spared Bernard Baran from spending twenty-one years in a high-security state prison. He was a free man when he died suddenly at age forty-nine, on September 1, 2014, but he had lived behind bars for the greater part of his adult life after being wrongfully convicted of raping several preschool children at the Early Childhood Development Center in Pittsfield, Massachusetts, where he had worked as a teacher's assistant. It took almost twenty years of post-conviction proceedings to prove, through evidence the prosecutors possessed all along, that the children's testimony had been made up, with considerable assistance from the investigation and prosecution team, to obtain Baran's indictment and conviction. Bernard Baran had not harmed the children at all.

The case had all the hallmarks of a legal nightmare. It was the ultimate public spectacle, fueled by public outrage and fanned by pervasive media attention. The 1985 Massachusetts jury trial that resulted in Baran's conviction was described by the state appeals court in 2009 as "notorious."[6] Trial had followed indictment by a mere three months, an extraordinarily short time for a lawyer to prepare to defend such a complex and emotional case. The burden of proof seems to fall on the defendant to prove his innocence in cases like this, and Baran's problems were further exacerbated by a mistake his mother had made in hiring his trial lawyer. Instead of the one she intended, she retained someone with a similar name who turned out to be a largely dysfunctional alcoholic, and she paid him less than a thousand dollars. Baran had essentially no legal defense at trial.

Convicted in the Massachusetts Superior Court on eight counts of rape and indecent assault and battery on a child under the age of fourteen, Baran was sentenced to concurrent life sentences. His conviction was affirmed by the appeals court in 1986. The trial lawyer had failed to preserve any issues for appeal, and the Massachusetts Supreme Judicial Court, facing no viable appeal issues in the trial record, refused to grant further appellate review. This seemed to be the end of the line for Bernard Baran. He was destined to spend the rest of his life in prison.

Fortunately for Baran, a group of his supporters, led by a civil liberties organization headquartered in Massachusetts, the National Center for Reason and Justice,[†] brought the case to the attention of two talented and dogged Boston criminal defense lawyers, John G. Swomley and Eric Tennen. They entered the case in 2000 and then enlisted Silverglate to work with them in investigating and seeking a new trial for Baran. These efforts were undertaken largely as a result of longstanding rumors that the child witnesses, who were between two and four years of age, might have been influenced in their testimony by highly suggestive interrogation techniques developed by self-proclaimed experts and known to have been used in similar cases around the country.[‡] It was a notorious era of social panic over an imagined epidemic of child sex abuse, and dozens of people went to prison for long terms as a result. In many states, day-care workers and others who had been convicted and incarcerated were later vindicated when the suggestive questioning of the children in response to social hysteria was uncovered.[†] Es-

---

† The National Center for Reason and Justice is a nonprofit charitable organization, recognized as such by the Internal Revenue Service. Silverglate was involved in the creation of the group and has served on its board of advisors since its inception.

‡ For instance, in New Jersey, Margaret Kelly Michaels, a twenty-four-year-old former teacher at the Wee Care Day Nursery in Maplewood, was prosecuted in 1988 with the assistance of an "abuse expert" who built her testimony around a list of "behavioral indicators" that she claimed were indicative of sex abuse in young children. California in 1983 gave the world the notorious McMartin preschool case. The State of Washington in 1994 prosecuted Robert Devereaux and others in the now-infamous "sex ring" that prosecutors claimed was run out of Devereaux's house and elsewhere in the town of Wenatchee. Multiple members of the Pentecostal Church of God House of Prayer in Wenatchee were charged as well. Several such cases occurred in Massachusetts, home to world-class educational and scientific institutions supposedly versed in the rational values of the Enlightenment and in the precepts of scientific method. Bernard Baran's young age and exceedingly gentle demeanor made his case particularly poignant.

sentially, false memories had been implanted into highly malleable and suggestible young minds.

Baran was a particularly apt target for the prosecutors, since he was openly gay at a time (the mid-1980s) and a place (culturally conservative Western Massachusetts) in which homosexuality was the object of considerable prejudice, and he was working in a job (day-care center) where the mere suggestion of a staff member's being gay was certain to arouse suspicions and parental concern. So it was no great surprise to either the news media or the citizens of Pittsfield when Baran was indicted.

Prosecutors admitted that the children had been interrogated by the district attorney's prosecution team. Importantly, these interrogations were videotaped. To avoid requiring the children to appear in person at the grand jury proceedings, however, the prosecutors showed *excerpts* from the interviews to the grand jurors who would indict Baran. These excerpts were preserved and were always available for review.

As the new defense team expected, these snippets from the taped interrogation sessions showed questions being put to the children, and the children responding that, yes, Baran did perform on them the various sexual acts alluded to by the interrogators. But what these excerpts did *not* disclose was that, *prior* to the grand jury proceedings, the children had been questioned by interrogation teams composed of parents, social service investigators, police officers, therapists, rape crisis center workers, and prosecutors. Baran's post-conviction legal team suspected that the *unedited* interrogation tapes, from which the accusatory snippets had been culled, would show that the children's damning and detailed accusations against Baran may have been prompted by the same suggestive

---

† For example, Harold Grant Snowden, an officer in the South Miami Police Department, was convicted in 1984 of molesting children under the care of his wife, and he served twelve years of five consecutive life terms before an appeals court overturned the conviction. He was prosecuted by Janet Reno, who would go on to become the United States attorney general in the Clinton administration. See Dorothy Rabinowitz, *No Crueler Tyrannies: Accusation, False Witness, and Other Terrors of Our Times* (New York: Free Press, 2004).

techniques being widely used by police, prosecutors, nurses, and social workers at the time.

Legal counsel thus naturally launched their effort to overturn the conviction by requesting that the district attorney, Gerard Downing, review his file to locate the unexcerpted, unexpurgated interview tapes. Baran's counsel strongly suspected that if they could learn the details of how Downing's predecessor Daniel Ford (later to become a state superior court judge) and his team had interrogated the children, the core of the allegations might well fall apart—as was happening in similar cases in many other states. Baran's original judge, William W. Simons, had retired in 1993, and the judge subsequently assigned to the case, Francis Fecteau, granted the defense's motion and ordered Downing to produce the original, unedited, unexcerpted tapes.

Yet despite repeated requests by the defense, bolstered by repeated production orders issued by Judge Fecteau, Downing insisted that his repeated searches for the original tapes were unsuccessful. This pattern of denial went on for over four years.

Finally, in December 2003, David Capeless took over the case as district attorney upon the sudden death of Downing, who suffered a fatal heart attack while shoveling snow from his driveway. It did not take Capeless long to find the full versions of the tapes that had so long eluded his predecessor, and he produced them to the defense in September 2004.

As expected, the tapes were virtually proof positive that the children's testimony had been manipulated, shaped, or wholly created by the questioners and implanted into the highly suggestible minds of the tots—who initially denied that they had been abused. The tapes established that Baran had been deprived of effective assistance of trial counsel as required by the state[7] and federal[8] constitutions. They also showed his actual innocence, and exposed likely violations of the prosecutors' legal and ethical obligations to produce *Brady* evidence.

Baran's post-conviction lawyers immediately realized they were almost certain to win Baran a new trial and, eventually, exoneration. They were granted the new trial in 2006, and Baran was released on bond after more than two decades in prison. Ultimately, the court dismissed the charges, but did it—as so often happens—in a way that protected the prosecutor.[9]

In fact, Daniel Ford, the prosecutor who was now a judge, had likely hidden from Baran's trial lawyer the original, unexcerpted tapes of the highly suggestive interviews of the children (an accusation which, fairness requires be said, Judge Ford adamantly denies, claiming that he turned the tapes over to Baran's trial lawyer, who did not use them at trial).

All in all, it was a delicate balancing act for Judge Fecteau and the state appeals court to grant Baran his freedom but stop short of turning over all the rocks to expose the worms writhing beneath. In May 2009, the appeals court unanimously affirmed the judge's tossing of the guilty verdict. The district attorney, David Capeless, wisely chose to forgo further appeal and retrial, and instead dismissed the indictment. At last, Bernard Baran was free.

Yet as in virtually every other case of which we are aware, there was no reckoning for the major actors in the unfathomably tragic deprivation of due process and loss of liberty that Baran suffered. The former district attorney, Gerard Downing, died before anybody could take him to task for failing to locate and turn over the damning unedited interview tapes for four years despite Judge Fecteau's repeated production orders. The trial prosecutor, Daniel Ford, was on the bench at the time Baran was freed, and the courts declined to examine his conduct at all.[†]

Some observers will say that "the system worked," since Baran was fully free when Capeless chose neither to appeal nor to retry the case. But that's a very debatable proposition. If indeed the system *eventually* worked for Baran, it took a quintessential act of God—a

---

† In theory, proof that Ford—by then a superior court judge—had knowingly and intentionally deprived a criminal defendant of clearly exculpatory evidence while he was a prosecutor could have resulted in disciplinary proceedings against him.

snowstorm and a fatal heart attack—to free a man who should never have been charged in the first place. And the trial prosecutor—by then a sitting state judge—did not have to respond, at least in any public forum, to hard questions concerning his conduct.[10] There must be a better way to ensure justice at the time of a trial, and to ensure adequate post-conviction review when justice at the trial level misfires. And, not so incidentally, there should be reliable mechanisms for disciplining prosecutors who stray, even if and when they later become judges, which prosecutors disproportionately do.

Sadly, Baran's case is but one of many in which prosecutors' *Brady* violations have eventually been discovered. It happened in the Michael Morton case in Texas, in the Duke lacrosse case in North Carolina, and in the Ted Stevens case in Washington, D.C., to name just a few of the more famous (or infamous) ones. Each of the present authors has described the government's appalling conduct in hiding exculpatory evidence in the case of Stevens, former United States senator, in our previous books: Silverglate in *Three Felonies a Day*, and Powell in *Licensed to Lie*, which also includes many more irrefutable examples. There are undoubtedly far more cases where *Brady* violations are never discovered.

•   •   •

How do we fix the problem? For an immediate, no-cost solution, every judge in the country should enter a *Brady* order like Judge Emmet G. Sullivan has done to solidify the government's responsibility in a form that can be enforced immediately by contempt charges.[†] Secondly, Congress and every state legislature should adopt clear, sweeping, unequivocal rules codifying the broadest all-encompassing *Brady* obligations, so there will be no doubt that the prosecution must do everything in its power to avoid the conviction of an innocent person.

---

† Judge Sullivan's order and a more rigorous order drafted by Powell are included in the Appendices.

Prosecutors must be required to disclose all evidence that is favorable to the defense—whether it proves actual innocence, impeaches a government witness, mitigates the sentence, or leads to other information helpful to the defendant. Such information should be produced by the prosecution regardless of whether it is itself admissible in evidence or whether the prosecutor views it as "material" to the defense; that is for the defense to determine. Moreover, the prosecution should be required to turn over the actual documents and statements, including notes—not summaries—except in cases where withholding them is plausibly necessary to protect the life of a witness, as decided by the court, not the government.

Some state court systems have adopted criminal discovery rules and procedures that aim to reduce the instances in which convictions are obtained notwithstanding the existence of evidence favorable to the defense but unknown to defense counsel. For example, North Carolina has adopted an "open-file" discovery statute[11] in response to the prosecutorial atrocities of the Duke lacrosse case, and Texas has done likewise[12] as a consequence of the Michael Morton case.

Florida has adopted a system of *reciprocal* discovery, in which a defendant can opt into a system where certain discovery procedures would be binding on both the prosecutor and the defense counsel.[13] While many defense attorneys would object to having to disclose the details of their defense to the other side, the Florida reciprocal system does hold out the promise of reducing not only surprise, but also the opportunities for false convictions.[14]

Under the Florida system, a prosecutor must supply a list of witnesses and of "all persons known to the prosecutor to have information that may be relevant" to the case, along with written exhibits, written or recorded statements of witnesses or codefendants, the defendant's grand jury testimony, if any, material information provided by confidential informants, electronic surveillance, products of searches and seizures, and the like. A judge has the authority to restrict, or redact, certain categories of disclosures—to protect other ongoing investigations, for example. In turn, the defendant would be subject to a reciprocal obligation, although the judge might limit a disclosure order directed to the defendant because of "constitutional limitations." And if a confidential informant is going to "be produced at a hearing or trial," then his identity must be disclosed.

The most revolutionary aspect of Florida's system is the right of either side to take depositions—oral interrogations of witnesses under oath with a stenographer or videographer present to record the proceedings—of the other side's witnesses. Such depositions of parties and witnesses have long been a staple of *civil* litigation. Some witnesses may be deposed via telephone, and not under oath, although their statements may be used to impeach their trial testimony if it differs from their telephonic interview.

Congress and the states should go even further. We need a provision that enables a defendant's lawyer in a state or federal criminal case to make an *ex parte* application to the judge, and upon a showing of appropriate cause appoint a neutral party to examine the prosecutor's file without advance notice. If the *Brady* rule is to be given any true meaning, prosecutors should be constantly aware of the fact that at any time a surreptitious violation of a solemn obligation of the state might be uncovered, with serious professional and perhaps other consequences for violations. Put more succinctly, the impunity and immunity that too often attach to violations of *Brady* obligations should end. Justice should not be a game at all—much less one of hide-and-seek or Go Fish.

• • •

Judges are notoriously reluctant to criticize, much less to penalize prosecutors for misconduct when they are caught withholding exculpatory evidence, yet some do recognize that violations of *Brady* obligations require a stern response. A prime example is Alex Kozinski, the former chief judge of the U.S. Court of Appeals for the Ninth Circuit, now retired.

In 2015, Judge Kozinski published an article in the *Georgetown Law Journal Annual Review of Criminal Procedure*,[15] in which he lays down a veritable challenge to the profession. After reviewing a number of areas in the criminal law where the presumption of innocence is undermined—fallible DNA evidence and other scientific tests (for example, fingerprint evidence), unreliable human memory, false confessions—he launches into a dissection of the mythology that "prosecutors play fair." In his discussion of the duty to disclose exculpatory evidence, Kozinski notes that "there is reason to doubt that prosecutors comply with these obligations fully." He criticizes the notion that it should be up to prosecutors to determine whether exculpatory material is sufficiently "material" to warrant turning it over. "Beyond that," writes Kozinski, "we have what I have described elsewhere as an epidemic of *Brady* violations abroad in the land."[16]

Subsequently, Judge Kozinski filed a published opinion in an appeal from a district court's denial of *habeas corpus* relief in a criminal case, *Frost v. Gilbert*,[17] in which he excoriated the state prosecutor responsible for a serious alleged *Brady* violation. Even though Kozinski agreed with the district judge that the petitioner was not entitled to relief due to the harsh procedural restrictions that govern federal *habeas corpus* law, he went on to accuse the state prosecutor of engaging in misconduct that the judge found "most troubling." For one thing, wrote Kozinski, the prosecutor withheld "evidence of [a government witness's] domestic-violence plea deal and...permitt[ed] [a witness] to lie on the stand." This, wrote the judge, was "a deliberate tactic rather than an oversight." And when the *habeas* petitioner "doggedly requested" the withheld information, "the [prosecutor's] office stonewalled." The judge added: "So far as we are aware, the individuals involved have never been held to account for their conduct." Kozinski and the minority of the appellate panel who agreed with him on this point named the prosecutors in the office responsible for these violations.

But in a scenario that is disturbingly common among judges addressing *Brady* violations, while the appellate panel unanimously agreed to affirm the district court's dismissal of the *habeas* petition, only a minority of the judges signed on to that portion of Judge Kozinski's opinion that took the prosecutors to task. Five members of the court called the accusatory portion of the Kozinski opinion "an imprudent exercise of . . . judicial power." (These five judges were not, it should be noted, saying that Kozinski had his facts wrong— only that he was "imprudent" in going beyond the narrow confines of his judicial review duties in that case.) And while they were at it, these five judges complained that the *habeas* petitioner, Mr. Frost, had already taken too much of the judiciary's time, since his claims were "procedurally defaulted" under the terms and intentions of the Antiterrorism and Effective Death Penalty Act of 1996. They reminded the reader that AEDPA was enacted by Congress "to conserve judicial resources, avoid piecemeal litigation, and eliminate delays in the federal habeas review process."[18] And they went on to underscore, lest it go unnoticed, that the section of Judge Kozinski's opinion criticizing the prosecutors "is not the judgment of this court" since that part of the opinion, and that part alone, failed to garner majority support.[19]

We need more judges like Kozinski who are willing to hold the government accountable and call out prosecutors for their misconduct. Unfortunately, few mechanisms exist to hold prosecutors accountable when they violate their *Brady* obligations.

Some states have begun to recognize that the absence of institutional oversight erodes faith in the system. New York is one such state. The legislature in Albany introduced bills to establish a commission that will oversee, investigate, and discipline instances of prosecutorial misconduct. Governor Andrew Cuomo signed the latest version into law in March 2019.[20] The commission is modeled on the accountability commissions that oversee judges in all fifty states. Of course, such a commission by itself would not prevent all *Brady* violations from occurring, but it certainly would aid justice in combination with other reforms. Further, conviction integrity units are beginning to be created in different offices around the country to review and remedy potential false convictions.

• • •

The legions of defendants wrongfully convicted in state and federal courts, due to the absence of adequate mechanisms for enforcing the *Brady* exculpatory evidence and other such rules, have occasioned numerous articles, studies, and proposals for solving the problem.[21] But such efforts rarely amount to more than a flash in the pan, lasting only as long as a spectacular or high-visibility case raises public outrage on the issue, then evaporating when public, judicial, and media attention wanes. When high-profile people of public importance become victims, however, reform efforts seem to be more vigorous.

Such was the case when Senator Ted Stevens was indicted for allegedly lying on his Senate ethics forms concerning his home remodeling. The case was sketchy at best, and the defense team of Brendan Sullivan, Rob Cary, and Simon Latcovich from Williams & Connolly caught the prosecution in one *Brady* violation after another. Finally, a few months after the verdict of guilty on seven counts had caused Stevens to lose his 2008 reelection bid by only a few thousand votes, thus altering the balance of power in the Senate, a young FBI agent broke ranks with his superiors and filed a whistleblower complaint—revealing that prosecutors had withheld evidence favorable to Stevens, along with numerous other instances of misconduct. The trial judge, Emmet G. Sullivan, exploded and held the original prosecution team in contempt, triggering the appointment of new prosecutors, who found significant *Brady* evidence within a few weeks. There was nothing left to do but dismiss the case. To save face, the newly appointed attorney general, Eric Holder, moved to do so "in the interest of justice."[22]

Judge Sullivan set aside the guilty verdict in April 2009. Still irate, he named a veteran D.C. lawyer, Henry Schuelke, to investigate the Department of Justice and its conduct, sending shockwaves through the department. Schuelke's investigation resulted in a 500-plus-page report excoriating the department. Schuelke found "systematic, intentional and pervasive" misconduct in the

Public Integrity Section that had prosecuted Stevens. Further, he found that the trial was "permeated by the systematic concealment of significant exculpatory evidence," which, if properly disclosed to the defense, would likely have resulted in a different verdict.

Following the corrupt prosecution of Senator Stevens, there was a massive bipartisan effort to pass legislation called the Fairness in Disclosure of Evidence Act. Six senators, three from each party, planned the introduction of this important legislation to coincide with the public release of the Schuelke Report. Yet despite the support of every bar association, the ACLU, the National Association of Criminal Defense Lawyers, the National Chamber of Commerce, the NAACP, and other significant legal organizations, the bill never made it out of committee. Why? It was opposed by our now ironically named Department of Justice—and that killed it.

Despite the government's blatant misconduct throughout the investigation and trial of Stevens, prosecutors escaped relatively unscathed. While the Schuelke Report found that at least two prosecutors had intentionally withheld *Brady* material, it concluded that the government could not bring a criminal contempt of court case against those individuals because the trial judge never issued a clear order that required the prosecution to disclose the exculpatory information. The offending prosecutors, it seemed, had escaped by taking advantage of what critics of the legal system often call "a technicality."

Judge Sullivan has attempted to remedy that problem in his courtroom, and he has encouraged judges across the country to do the same. He now enters clear and precise *Brady* orders as soon as he receives a case on his docket.† Indeed, when he was assigned the case recently brought by Robert Mueller, the special counsel, against Michael Flynn, Sullivan entered an order that required

---

† Judge Sullivan's standing *Brady* order and one drafted by Sidney Powell are included in the Appendices.

the Office of Special Counsel to produce all *Brady* evidence, even though Flynn had entered a guilty plea.

Several of the highest-ranking prosecutors left the Department of Justice before the Schuelke Report came out. Unsurprisingly, they found cushy private sector positions.[23] Ultimately, two prosecutors were assessed suspensions of fourteen and thirty days, and one of them served one day of it before the suspensions were reversed by the internal Department of Justice review board for failure to follow department procedures in imposing discipline. Reports are that three of the original Stevens prosecutors still work in the department.

To call this an outrage is an understatement. A prosecutor's intentional suppression of *Brady* evidence is tantamount to obstruction of justice and in some cases amounts to subornation of perjury. Those are felony offenses for which such prosecutors readily prosecute other people. If the prosecutors can break the law with immunity and impunity like this, then there is no law. Prosecutors who are found to have committed intentional *Brady* violations should be terminated immediately. That is the bare minimum acceptable for any office that purports to seek justice—not convictions.

• • •

What links the stories of a long-serving United States senator and a Massachusetts day-care worker, is this: Ted Stevens and Bernard Baran—like countless others—were both victims of an adversarial discovery system and of a culture that completely shields prosecutors from accountability. In the federal government's prosecution of Senator Stevens and in the Massachusetts state case against Baran, prosecutors' withholding of evidence favorable to the defense altered the course of the trial and the life of an innocent man. In both cases, it was ultimately luck that delivered some semblance of justice.

An open-file discovery system—working in tandem with pretrial discovery committees, standing disclosure orders, and consolidated files—would go a long way in keeping innocent people out of prison. Indeed, Judge Emmet Sullivan was right when he said during Stevens's trial that "people should not have to rely on luck to get justice."

Acts of God have their place in life, but the courtroom should operate in accordance with open legal procedures that ensure justice. A defendant should not have to rely on the serendipity by which the truth might emerge miraculously, but far too late to prevent an egregious injustice that sends an innocent man to prison or changes the balance of power in the United States Senate through a criminal conviction that is later overturned. Some cases of this kind are spectacular and well known. In countless others, the truth never does emerge.

CHAPTER FOUR

WHAT DOES THE LAW REQUIRE OF US?

The Conundrum of Criminal Intent

I t's the morning of election day. People around the country gather at their local polling places to cast their ballots. There is a sense of excitement as citizens emerge from the booths, having exercised a vital part of their civic duty for another cycle. One voter, a navy lieutenant, takes her daughter by the hand and starts to head back home. She is stopped by a young, enthusiastic student who asks if she'd like to take part in an exit poll. He hands her the questionnaire, which includes a question about whom she voted for, of course. She fills in the answers, folds it up, and drops it into a secure box.

Little does this voter know that she has just turned the student pollster into a criminal, because it is a federal crime to poll a member of the armed forces.[1] The worst part is that the pollster doesn't have to know that the law exists, or that the voter is in the armed services, to be guilty.

• • •

All crimes are made up of elements. For a person to be guilty of a crime, the government must prove beyond a reasonable doubt that each element of the crime is met. Traditionally, the elements of a crime were placed under the headings of *actus reus*, Latin for "guilty act," and *mens rea*, or "guilty mind." But the age-old requirement that a person has to act with a guilty mind to violate a law has slowly been disappearing. Unfortunately for our student pollster, the only elements of the relevant crime are that the voter was a member of the armed forces and that the pollster asked for information about the voter's choice. There is no statutory requirement that the pollster have intended to gather information on servicemembers.

This problem is everywhere in our criminal law. It is a multifaceted problem arising from the combination of too many laws, too many regulations that can be incorporated into vague criminal statutes, and too many overzealous prosecutors. What the common law calls *mens rea*—that is, the mental state required to have criminal intent—is missing from a whole range of crimes today, and overly creative prosecutors have come to use such statutes as a means to target those they dislike.[†] The clever operatives choose the statutes with the lowest requirement of criminal intent and try to shoehorn the facts into the elements of those easier-to-prove violations. Then they invoke the full might and power of the United States to grind defendants to dust.

An egregious example of this practice is *United States v. Rafiekian*, a case filed by the Office of Special Counsel in the Eastern District of Virginia. Driven by Brandon Van Grack (a hot-headed lawyer and Weissmann wannabe),[‡] prosecutors used this creative, unprecedented, weak case to cement the guilty plea of Lieutenant General Michael Flynn (Ret.) as he was about to appear before Judge Emmet Sullivan on December 18, 2018, for what was scheduled to be his sentencing.

On the eve of Flynn's appearance, the prosecutors unsealed the

---

† In 1940, Attorney General Robert H. Jackson warned of this problem in his famous speech, "The Federal Prosecutor," quoted in the Preface.

‡ To understand Andrew Weissmann and why this is a problem, one must read *Licensed to Lie*.

indictment of two businessmen (one from Turkey) who had participated in a consulting business transaction with Flynn. They charged the two with conspiracy to act as an agent of a foreign government and to make willfully false statements in the Flynn Intel Group's filing under the Foreign Agents Registration Act (FARA), and with the substantive offense of being foreign agents under 18 U.S.C. § 951—as if they had acted at the direction and control of a foreign government, essentially committing some kind of espionage. These charges subjected them to possible imprisonment of fifteen years, for a ninety-day project that resulted in nothing more than the publication of an opinion piece in *The Hill* on December 8, 2016.

Both the purported FARA violation and section 951 have rarely been used against anyone, much less for facially innocent conduct that no one would think was unlawful, and in a very complex area of the law. In fact, the defendant Bijan Rafiekian and General Flynn had spent more than $350,000 with the "white-shoe" firm of Covington & Burling, hiring one of the leading FARA experts to make the Flynn Intel Group's filing. Ironically, writing and publishing the opinion piece is also conduct protected by the First Amendment. That doesn't matter to prosecutors for whom the ends justify the means, and who aim to intimidate and convict someone they want to destroy.[2] In this case, the prosecutors chose section 951 because of its lesser *mens rea* requirement.[3]

Crimes are often divided into different types according to the element of intent. If a law requires that a guilty person only intended to perform the illegal conduct but not to cause the result of that conduct, then that is a *general intent* crime. If, on the other hand, a law requires that the guilty person intended both the conduct and the result, that is a *specific intent* crime. To see the difference, think about manslaughter versus murder. If a person's intentional actions lead unintentionally to someone's death, that is manslaughter. If a person intends to cause someone's death through the actions taken, that is murder. The fact that more people might be guilty of manslaughter than murder doesn't offend our sense of morality.

We generally think manslaughter deserves less punishment than murder.

But the question of intent has led to a lot of confusion, and it is the subject of considerable ink spilled by judges, legislators, and lawyers. In the 1950s and 1960s, the American Law Institute set out to define the different mental states required for different types of crimes, and the result was the Model Penal Code. This is a set of example statutes designed to help legislatures pass thoughtful criminal laws.

The Model Penal Code defined four different mental states that a criminal statute could require: purposely, knowingly, recklessly, and negligently. Acting purposely means a person intends to do the act or cause the result. Acting knowingly is a question of whether a person knows that the action is the kind of thing a law condemns, or that it might cause a result the law prohibits. A person acts recklessly by doing something that is outside the bounds of normal law-abiding behavior and consciously disregarding the risk that a bad result may follow. Acting negligently is the lowest form of *mens rea*; all it takes is that a person acted without seeing that a risk would exist.

There is another type of crime, though: the *strict liability* offense. Strict liability means that one doesn't need to have any knowledge of the law or any intent to act unlawfully. Traffic offenses are essentially strict liability: for the most part, if you speed, it doesn't matter that you didn't know what the speed limit is or that you were exceeding it. Similarly, selling alcohol or cigarettes to an underage person is often strict liability, regardless of whether the salesman knows the buyer's age. Our Espionage Act includes prohibitions of some conduct that amounts to virtual strict liability, but people in our government who have security clearances are schooled in the importance of maintaining our government's secrets in the interest of our national security, which minimizes their risk of running afoul of the law.

In our example of the student pollster, the statute does include the word "intent," and at first glance it seems to require some particular mental state. But the list of things that come after the word "intent" makes it meaningless. The prohibition on polling members of the armed forces defines a "poll" as any request for a voter's information with the intent of compiling it for reporting or publishing, or "for the personal use of the person making the request." So, the student pollster could be getting paid for the work or just writing a paper for a college class. It isn't quite strict liability, but it is an example of how the terms that impart a *mens rea* element to a crime in a statute are not always meaningful. There must be some intent, but it can be any intent, and it certainly does not have to be criminal intent.

This is why we need *mens rea* reform, to bring the law into accord with the United States Constitution. The rights enshrined in the Constitution largely concern individual liberty, and most of the language in the Bill of Rights focuses on ways in which individual liberty may not be constrained by legislative or government action. Think about the opening words of the First Amendment: "Congress shall make no law...." Therefore, when individual liberty *is* constrained by law, the principles upon which this nation was founded demand that the individual be aware of the constraint.

• • •

As the regulatory state began to expand a century ago, criminal law became a rapidly burgeoning means to control behavior. This was particularly true, for example, in food and drug laws. In the famous case of *United States v. Dotterweich* (1943),[4] a manager of a company that purchased pharmaceuticals in bulk and then repackaged them for sale was found guilty under a law imposing strict liability on anyone responsible for shipping "misbranded or adulterated" drugs in interstate commerce. The Supreme Court held that this statute was valid, even though it had no element of intent and imposed strict liability on the manager. Justice Felix Frankfurter wrote:

Balancing relative hardships, Congress has preferred to place it upon those who have at least the opportunity of informing themselves of the existence of conditions imposed for the protection of consumers before sharing in illicit commerce, rather than to throw the hazard on the innocent public who are wholly helpless.[5]

In fact, the Buffalo Pharmaceutical Company that Dotterweich worked for was not at all responsible for the bad conduct in the case. The manufacturers they got the drugs from had made a mistake on their own labels, causing Dotterweich's company to pass along the drugs with the mistake. Most importantly, the government never had to prove that Dotterweich himself knew either that the drugs were mislabeled or that they were sent into interstate commerce. He was guilty without having any intent to break any law or even knowing that the drugs were mislabeled. Is this fair or just?

Crimes of this kind are generally called "public welfare offenses," and the justification for making them crimes is always similar to Dotterwiech's case: some perceived danger to the public outweighs the rights of the accused. These crimes are not like assault, arson, or murder, where the wrongful nature of the act is obvious; these are crimes simply because the government says so. In the language of the law, crimes that are obviously wrong are *mala in se*, literally meaning "bad in itself." On the other hand, crimes that are based only on a pronouncement of the government, making otherwise apparently innocent conduct punishable by fines or jail, are called *malum prohibitum*, forbidden wrongs.

Less than ten years after Dotterweich's conviction was upheld by the Supreme Court, another statute without a *mens rea* element came up for review, in 1952. A scrap metal dealer named Joe Morissette was hunting deer in the woods near Flint, Michigan, when he came upon some spent bomb casings, about forty inches long and eight inches across. There was no one around for miles, and Joe thought these casings were abandoned property. So he loaded them into his truck, took them to a friend to be flattened out, and sold them at a scrap market in town. He made $84 on the deal—and wound up with a two-month prison sentence and a $200 fine.

Why? Well, what Joe Morissette didn't know was that the minute he put those bomb casings in his truck to sell them later, he was guilty of stealing government property. The Air Force had dropped those shells in the woods some years before as simulated bombs. Morissette didn't notice a few old signs warning that this was (or had been) a bombing range, but he saw a pile of rusty shells that had been cleared away from what used to be the targets. They may have been there for years, but as far as the government was concerned, Morissette still should have known that the shells were not abandoned.

The Supreme Court, to Morissette's relief, disagreed and struck down his conviction. Justice Robert Jackson wrote:

> The contention that an injury can amount to a crime only when inflicted by intention is no provincial or transient notion. It is as universal and persistent in mature systems of law as belief in freedom of the human will and a consequent ability and duty of the normal individual to choose between good and evil.[6]

Decades after *Morissette*, the Supreme Court continues to tackle statutes that are missing *mens rea* elements. There has long been debate, for example, over a law that takes away the Second Amendment rights of certain groups of people, including drug users, persons previously convicted of felonies, and undocumented immigrants.[7] This law is often referred to as "felon-in-possession," but it actually swallows up a much broader class of people. Anyone deemed to fall into those categories found with a firearm is guilty of a federal crime, without even using the gun to do anything. Though the statute says that one must "knowingly" violate the law to be guilty, it has always been unclear what someone must "know" to violate this law "knowingly." In a 7-to-2 decision in June 2019, the Court held that someone must know he possessed the gun *and* know that he fits into one of the prohibited categories to be guilty.[8]

Another example comes from a case where a young man posted some explicit song lyrics to his Facebook page while he was going through a breakup.[9] His estranged wife saw the posts and thought they were intended to threaten her. Prosecutors filed charges against him under a statute making it illegal to transmit threats, and the jury was instructed that he only had to be "negligent" about the fact that someone else could have seen his words as a threat. Claiming this was a violation of his First Amendment rights, he took the case to the Supreme Court. Seven justices agreed that it isn't enough that another person might consider the words threatening; to be guilty of this crime, someone must communicate a threat intentionally. Chief Justice Roberts wrote: "Federal criminal liability generally does not turn solely on the results of an act without considering the defendant's mental state."[10]

•   •   •

Decisions like these are baby steps forward, but they aren't enough. Judge-made law is subject to the whims of judges. Durable reform comes from legislative solutions, but Congress doesn't seem to pick up on the Supreme Court's repeated warnings about the need for criminal intent in criminal law. We must halt the bipartisan march toward controlling behavior by overcriminalizing conduct and prison-bursting politics. We need to stop rendering our citizens subject to the whims of prosecutors who can prosecute anyone with whom they disagree, because with so many laws they can find something to pin on anyone.

Each side has its own ideas about how to solve the nation's problems through harsh criminal penalties. These ideas are implemented by the passing of new laws that make more and more actions criminal. The cycle has brought us to the point of having nearly 5,000 federal criminal statutes on the books and over 300,000 federal regulations that impose criminal penalties.[11]

These criminal laws often have vague language, or none at all, about what someone has to know to be guilty.[12] As a consequence, people are accused, and convicted, of crimes they didn't know they were committing for facially innocent conduct they did not know the law prohibited. Somehow, a nation built on freedom and liberty has managed to end up with citizens who live in growing apprehension of our "criminal justice" system and see it as completely broken.

We need drastic reform to break the cycle, so that innocent people are not subjected to crushing abuse by our "criminal justice" system. Harsh criminal laws are often adopted with bipartisan support by misguided lawmakers, so reforming those laws should be a nonpartisan effort. In particular, we need to fix the problem of *mens rea* in criminal law—an issue that Senator Orrin Hatch (now retired) diligently tried to address while he was in the Senate, as described below.

The problem is twofold: many new laws are written without any language at all on the mental state required, but when the language is included, it is often unclear as to what mental state is required for which elements of the law.[13] Think back to our student pollster: what does he have to know to be guilty? All the statute says about intent is that the request for the voter's information must be "made with the intent of compiling the result of the answers obtained,"[14] but as mentioned above, those results might be intended only for the personal use of the pollster—and how would he ever know that was wrong, much less illegal? Nothing else in the statute seems guided by any criminal intent requirement.

Justice Robert Jackson, in Joe Morissette's case, explained why many criminal laws in America didn't have any language about *mens rea*. He described how a sense of individualism meant that the necessity of proving both a guilty mind and a guilty action—the "concurrence of an evil-meaning mind with an evil-doing hand"— to convict someone was taken for granted.[15] While he seemed to accept that some public welfare offenses would always be strict liability crimes, Justice Jackson said clearly that for crimes like picking up rusty metal in the woods, the government must prove that you know your conduct is criminal.[16] Yet more than half a century later, with the knowledge that this missing element of criminal intent cannot be assumed and must be explicit, Congress has still not engaged in a process of meaningful *mens rea* reform.

A joint report from the National Association of Criminal Defense Lawyers and the Heritage Foundation in 2010 spearheaded a new initiative to make the necessary change. The report made five major recommendations to Congress:

1. Enact default rules of interpretation to ensure that *mens rea* requirements are adequate to protect against unjust conviction.
2. Codify the common-law rule of lenity, which grants defendants the benefit of doubt when Congress fails to legislate clearly.
3. Require judiciary committee oversight of every bill that includes criminal offenses or penalties.
4. Require detailed written justification for and analysis of all new federal criminalization.
5. Redouble efforts to draft every criminal offense clearly and precisely.[17]

The report closed by reminding Congress that because it is entrusted with defining criminal conduct, it has a duty to ensure that no one is criminally punished unless its own resources have been devoted to passing laws that are clearly and precisely defined.[18]

•　•　•

As is often the case, state governments, in their role as "laboratories of democracy,"[19] have provided Congress a blueprint for *mens rea* reform. Michigan and Ohio have seen successful bipartisan efforts to implement a default standard for criminal intent when statutes don't already contain one.

In Michigan, the reform was prompted in large part by outrage when Alan N. Taylor, the owner of a company that produces vital medical devices, faced thousands of dollars in fines for violating criminal penalties.[20] His crime? Slightly extending his company parking lot onto a protected wetland. The problem? He had no reason to know this area was a wetland. The topsoil had been stripped away more than a decade before, and the land had clearly been prepared for construction. A highway and a gas pipeline had recently been laid on adjacent land.[21] Taylor had absolutely no reason to know he was violating any laws, but he was convicted of two misdemeanors.

Because of a procedural technicality, he could not get relief from the appellate court.[22] The Michigan Supreme Court also denied his appeal, but in an unusual move, one of its justices wrote a special opinion with a word of warning:

> It is the responsibility of our Legislature to determine the state of mind required to satisfy the criminal statutes of our state, and the judiciary is ill-equipped when reviewing increasingly broad and complex criminal statutes to discern whether some *mens rea* is intended, for which elements of an offense it is intended, and what exactly that *mens rea* should be.[23]

The Michigan legislature responded to this call by passing a *mens rea* reform bill that instituted a default standard and required any future legislation intended to create a strict liability offense to say so explicitly.[24] The bill was signed into law in late 2015. This kind of reform can be expected to boost public confidence in criminal justice by limiting the application of criminal law to those who intend to commit a crime or have reason to know their conduct is unlawful before they engage in it.[25]

•   •   •

Luckily, there are many in Congress who recognize the problem of vague laws that make criminals of people who have no reason to think they are doing anything illegal, and some legislators are trying to reform such laws. Senators Orrin Hatch, Rand Paul, and Chuck Grassley (all Republicans) have championed *mens rea* reform as a central part of any attempt to overhaul the criminal justice system.[26] Building on prior efforts, Senators Hatch and Grassley introduced the *Mens Rea* Reform Act of 2018. This legislation would have done three main things:

- Create a National Criminal Justice Commission to identify any federal criminal laws lacking a *mens rea* element. The commission and Congress would have had five years to amend these laws.
- Give federal agencies six years to conduct a similar review of federal regulations. Any regulation remaining after six years without a specified *mens rea* standard would be invalid.
- Set a default "willfully" standard for any future criminal law unless Congress specifically set out another.[27]

As the senators described it: "Our bill will begin the work of clarifying the criminal law already on the books and will encourage Congress and federal agencies to be more careful when creating criminal penalties going forward."[28]

One of the easiest ways for Congress to end overcriminalization is to pass a simple statute providing that no regulation can be criminalized unless Congress specifically does so in 18 United States Code. Unfortunately, partisan politics and obstructionism have blocked this reform. Bipartisan criminal justice reform legislation passed in late 2018, called the First Step Act, did not include *mens rea* reform,[29] just as an unsuccessful compromise bill in 2015 had not.[30] In both instances, two Democratic senators, Richard Durbin and Sheldon Whitehouse, led the charge against its inclusion, the latter saying that adding *mens rea* reform to the bill "would make me a warrior against it."[31]

Curiously, the objection seems to be that the reform would do exactly what it is intended to do: subject fewer people to criminal penalties. The problem these Democrats have with such a prospect is that they think the people who would avoid criminal punishment are slimy corporate executives. Dick Durbin once said that *mens rea* reform "should be called the White Collar Criminal Immunity Act."[32] Liberal think tanks have released reports claiming that the reform would allow white-collar defendants to plead ignorance of the law, leave critical safety statutes unenforced, and create legal uncertainty.[33] Yet, the reforms are actually intended and designed to do the opposite: define statutory elements more precisely so that everyone knows what conduct is prohibited, thereby improving enforcement and creating stability and certainty.

The *Mens Rea* Reform Act of 2018 was in fact already informed by recommendations and compromises that commentators encouraged after the failed efforts in 2015. For example, the New York City Bar Association sent a detailed letter urging the very ideas that Senators Hatch and Grassley later incorporated for the National Criminal Justice Commission and the extended period for agencies to review their regulations.[34] Law professors from ivy-league schools made public pleas for the Democrats to participate and find compromise legislation.[35] Unfortunately, the 2018 *mens rea* proposal did not become part of the First Step Act, so another of the New York City Bar's recommendations will have to be followed: considering *mens rea* reform as a stand-alone legislative effort.

Do the critics have a point about disparate effects on criminal defendants of different categories? And if they do, what's the solution? Benjamin Levin, a criminal justice scholar and University of Colorado law professor, tackled these questions in an article published soon after the passage of the First Step Act. Here he discusses what he calls the "three core pathologies of U.S. criminal policy," namely:

1. a commitment to using criminal law as the default regulatory model;

2. a tendency to level up when faced with inequality (i.e., to punish the powerful defendant more, rather than punishing the powerless defendant less); and

3. the temptation for mass incarceration critics to make exceptions and support harsh treatment for particularly unsympathetic defendants.[36]

Professor Levin acknowledges that the bulk of criminal prosecutions are unlike our example of the student pollster. He also concedes that *mens rea* reform is narrowly focused and cannot cure all the ills of the criminal justice system, as no single reform can. "But it is not entirely clear," he writes, "why this critique would indicate that *mens rea* reform is a policy to be opposed, rather than a proposal that should be only one small piece of a larger, more ambitious reform agenda."[37]

Professor Levin's most powerful words, though, come in the context of what he calls "leveling up." This is the idea that when faced with one defendant punished too little and one punished too much, the right remedy is to punish the first one more and not the second one less. This is where the Democrats' objection comes in: when a defendant in a drug case gets a decades-long sentence and a defendant in a white-collar case gets only a fine, the impulse is to give the white-collar defendant more time. But as Levin points out, "Just because the politics of *mens rea* reform look different than the politics of three-strikes laws, the War on Drugs, or other often conservative-backed endeavors, this turn to criminal law [by "progressives"] should not be exempt from a critical eye."[38] When our answer to every social ill—whether the problem we see is on the streets or in the boardrooms—is to pass a new criminal law, we end up where we are: with 2.25 million people in prison or jail.[39]

• • •

Here's the truth: reforms that help one group in the short term can be used to benefit everyone in the long term. That's something the country learned from Ruth Bader Ginsburg. In the 1970s, when she was an ACLU lawyer arguing at the Supreme Court instead of the one making the decisions, her strategy was to find men who had suffered gender discrimination. In a series of cases, she dismantled unjust policies on spousal benefits and property inheritance. If she could explain how laws that favored women over men were bad, then she could establish a logically consistent position to justify eliminating laws that favored men over women. She was criticized by some on her own side for engaging in an effort that would backfire and not achieve her goals, but she was largely successful.[40]

We face the same problem with *mens rea* reform. Some on the left—specifically, an element in the Senate unwilling to compromise—are letting their own predilections about which type of crime should be punished more harshly impede their efforts at common-sense reform that would serve all Americans. Certainly, some people accused of economic or regulatory crimes—the majority of whom come from groups that are more affluent than those accused of other types of crime—may benefit from *mens rea* reforms. But that doesn't mean the benefits won't inure to everyone. These reforms are right because they are the right thing to do, not because of whom they will or won't benefit in the short term. After all, the same prosecutors that are—often rightly—accused of unfair or aggressive tactics in one context are enforcing the laws in all contexts. It is inconsistent to say that these prosecutors are good when they enforce some laws (financial crimes or environmental regulations) and bad when they enforce others (drug or gun laws).

Even if the critics are right, and *mens rea* reform would be good for those accused of white-collar crime, that does not mean it won't also be good for those accused of other kinds of crime. Why do we have a desire to punish white-collar defendants more harshly, rather than ease the burden of the state on all people accused of crime? Why would using criminal laws punitively to incarcerate "transgressors" be moral in some cases and not in others? Isn't it better that everyone who is not a danger to the community or a risk of flight be able to remain at home, living at his own expense (even if on home confinement), working to support his family, paying taxes and generally contributing to society, instead of costing taxpayers upward of $40,000 a year to be warehoused in a nonproductive cage? We can be much less creative in criminalizing conduct and more creative in how we punish true crimes and criminals without causing wasteful, needless, expensive, and counterproductive confinement.

Don't all those who are accused of crime deserve the same rights to have the elements of their alleged offense proved beyond a reasonable doubt? In fact, Justice Ginsburg herself agrees that certain financial crimes do require that someone act "willfully," as evidenced by her majority opinion in the Supreme Court case of *Ratzlaf v. United States.*[41] There, a defendant was charged under a statute that made it a crime to structure bank deposits just small enough to avoid reporting them. Justice Ginsburg invoked the statutory text and the common law "rule of lenity," which requires that an unclear statute be interpreted in favor of a criminal defendant, to find that Ratzlaf could not be guilty under this statute because the government had not proved his criminal intent.[42]

Criminal laws are not the best way to regulate society. The idea that we can make an "example" by prosecuting someone under a strict liability statute miscalculates what is communicated by punishment.[43] Let's assume, for the sake of argument, that punishment can communicate society's values appropriately. If our student pollster were arrested and charged, without knowing about the law against polling the military or even that the voter he approached was a servicemember, what would that communicate? Would it say that we are a society of laws, where individual liberty is protected? Granted, the jails are not overflowing with defendants like this, but if we are talking about the way that law can communicate ideas, then we must be as precise as possible. Individual liberty is about individuals, so whether one or one hundred or one thousand defendants are potentially exposed to criminal liability should make no difference. If our laws make criminals out of people with no criminal intent, then our system has failed.

Criminal punishment "represents the moral condemnation" of society, as the Supreme Court has said.[44] It changes lives and families forever. We should think long and hard about the circumstances and level of knowledge and intent that ought to be required for such condemnation and punishment to be imposed.

CHAPTER FIVE

PLEA BARGAINING

Dancing with the Devil

More than 95 percent of federal convictions now result from guilty pleas.[1] The precious Sixth Amendment right to trial by jury is all but gone. Countless Americans seem oblivious to one of the greatest abuses, outrages, and tragedies of our criminal justice system: innocent people being forced to plead guilty as a daily occurrence in federal district courts around the nation. Indeed, the Innocence Project alone has exonerated thirty-one people who spent a combined 150 years in prison on guilty pleas.[2]

That is only the tip of the proverbial iceberg. This horrific injustice is the result of federal and state lawmakers and judges conceding far too much power to prosecutors, with no remedies or accountability even for the prosecutors' deliberate, intentional misconduct. While this book focuses primarily on the federal system, most of the same problems exist in spades within the state systems.

The prosecutor now functions as prosecutor, judge, jury, and executioner. He has unfettered discretion, no supervision, and no limits. Most federal judges, who often were federal prosecutors at one point in their career, defer to him at every turn. As Jed Rakoff, a federal judge, opined in a seminal essay in the *New York Review of Books*, "it is the prosecutor, not the judge, who effectively exercises the sentencing power, albeit cloaked as a charging decision."[3]

Onerous federal sentencing guidelines also allow for abuse by prosecutors. Although they were rendered "non-binding" by the Supreme Court, federal judges rarely depart from them.[4] But prosecutors can stack charges and thereby ratchet up the guidelines to a term of life in prison for almost any factual scenario. They can bring so much force to bear against a defendant that he is compelled to plead guilty, even if he is innocent, to avoid spending decades or the rest of his life in prison.

To see how the plea-bargaining process works in practice, it is instructive to examine the case of Lieutenant General Michael Flynn (Ret.). Following Donald Trump's victory in the 2016 presidential election, General Flynn joined Trump's transition team to advise on national security issues, and upon Trump's inauguration, Flynn officially became the national security advisor.

General Flynn is the quintessential example of why the innocent plead guilty. He had barely unpacked his boxes in his new office in the White House when he received what he thought was a friendly phone call from Andrew McCabe, the FBI deputy director. McCabe asked to send a couple of agents over to the White House on January 24, 2017, to talk to Flynn. According to McCabe, he encouraged Flynn not to involve White House counsel. Flynn agreed.

The agents, who were investigating purported Russian interference in the 2016 election, came to question Flynn about his conversations with Sergey Kislyak, the Russian ambassador to the United States during Flynn's work on President-Elect Trump's transition team. Flynn knew the FBI had complete recordings and transcripts of the conversations in question, and those calls were lawful. He conducted them as part of his job in the transition to the new administration.

Flynn greeted the two FBI agents, Peter Strzok and Joe Pientka, like long-lost friends and colleagues, showing them around the White House. He talked about the long hours in the job, the pains of politics, life on the campaign trail, the president's knack for decorating, but the conversation always returned to his main preoccupation—the plague of terrorism. The agents asked a few questions about his meetings or conversations with Kislyak. He told them about one they did not know of, and they reminded him of one he had forgotten, but he recalled few details. After the meeting, both agents reported—in at least three debriefings that day—their belief that Flynn was telling the truth. They maintained that belief even to cries of "bullshit" from McCabe and the small, high-level group that had planned the ambush interview.

Two days later, the acting attorney general, Sally Yates—wingman to Attorney General Loretta Lynch during the final years of the Obama administration—was in the office of Don McGahn, White House counsel. She claimed Flynn was a risk because the Russians could blackmail him. How? That's still not clear. In talking with the Russian ambassador, Flynn did nothing illegal.[5] Everyone knew the calls were recorded. What information is shared within the White House is not the business of the FBI—nor are the foreign policy choices of the president. After the media hounded the new administration with reports that Flynn had lied to Vice President Pence about the substance of one of the calls, the president, advised by McGahn, accepted Flynn's resignation—effectively spilling Flynn's blood in the water for the sharks to attack.[6]

As soon as Robert Mueller was appointed special counsel in the spring of 2017 to investigate Russian interference in the 2016 election, Flynn was first in his crosshairs. James Comey, former FBI director, eventually admitted publicly that the FBI had opened an investigation on Flynn early in the campaign with no basis to do so—as the FBI did on three other American citizens. The FBI may have obtained a FISA warrant on Flynn (based on nothing) or reached his communications by virtue of the FISA warrant on Carter Page. The rabid prosecutors on Mueller's squad threatened the national hero with multiple counts in an indictment that would expose him to life in prison for himself, and they threatened to indict his son and send him to prison as well. The younger Flynn had a four-month-old baby. The prosecutors had already seized all the electronic devices of both men and grilled General Flynn for hours. And as Powell learned once she got into the case, his prior counsel had a serious conflict of interest—so egregious that even if Flynn had been fully informed of it early on, it could not be waived. They had prepared the FARA filing that the government insisted on using as leverage for charges and the plea.

Prosecutors' treatment of Flynn and threat to indict his son unless the elder Flynn pleaded guilty is not unique; it is standard operating procedure for the Department of Justice in white-collar cases—especially when Mueller's "pit bull" Andrew Weissmann is involved. Weissmann, Mueller's second-in-command in the Office of Special Counsel, is a studied practitioner of this form. In the Enron case, Weissmann indicted and imprisoned Andrew Fastow's wife, Lea, when he did not plead and cooperate on demand. Fastow decided not only to plead but to "sing and compose," to use Professor Alan Dershowitz's apt phrase.[†]

Weissmann is so adept at wielding threats against targets and family members that he has coerced people into pleading guilty to things that were not crimes. Two defendants in the Enron scandal whose cases are discussed in *Licensed to Lie* had to be allowed to withdraw their guilty pleas.[7] David Duncan, a partner at Arthur Andersen LLP, was allowed to withdraw his plea after he had testified for the government in the subsequent trial of the audit firm.[8] Richard Calger was allowed to withdraw his plea also.

General Flynn cooperated with the special counsel investigation from its inception, which he likely would have done under any

---

[†] Fastow, the actual architect of Enron's frauds, stole and pocketed millions of dollars from Enron through his illegal schemes. He spent thousands of hours "cooperating" with the government after he saw the light, and even though he and his protégé Michael Kopper had stolen the money, they got extremely light sentences, while others who stole nothing got sentences of up to twenty-four years.

circumstances. Nonetheless, he saw his legal fees quickly explode into seven figures. He had to sell his home in Alexandria to pay his legal fees and then ask the public to help with his legal defense fund as his fees mounted higher into the millions. Even relatively "well-heeled" citizens do not have the capacity to withstand a determined prosecutorial assault. Flynn had served in the military for thirty-three years, including five years in active combat. He did not qualify as "well-heeled."

Like so many others, as Judge Rakoff described, General Flynn felt compelled to take the plea deal offered to him: plead guilty to one count of making a false statement to the FBI agents, and continue to cooperate with the government, in exchange for which the government would recommend probation. The alternative was to risk spending the rest of his life in prison, suffering complete financial ruin, watching his son be prosecuted and sent to prison, and drowning in years of litigation—all in a process calculated to destroy one's entire family.

James Comey later boasted that he and Andrew McCabe, together with the two FBI agents, had essentially targeted and ambushed Flynn, eschewing normal procedures by sending agents to interview him without coordinating with the White House Counsel's Office. To laughter and applause from an audience at Manhattan's 92nd Street Y in December 2018, Comey described this tactic as "something we, I, probably wouldn't have done or maybe gotten away with in a more organized investigation, a more organized administration."[9]

Then, after almost two years of unimaginable stress for his entire family—each unit of which, up and down the generations, had multiple members who had served in the military—General Flynn had what he thought was going to be a sentencing hearing on December 18, 2018. He walked into Judge Emmet G. Sullivan's courtroom in Washington, D.C., with an appearance of some relief. The government had recently filed its sentencing memorandum, and it had recommended a sentence of probation for this hero who had served his country brilliantly in and out of combat for thirty-three years.

Federal judges usually accept the recommendation of the government in plea agreements, and everyone in attendance that day expected Judge Sullivan to enter that sentence in a relatively short and pro forma proceeding.

Powell, who later became counsel for Flynn, harbored a belief that Sullivan would call out the government for its violations of the *Brady* rule—that is, for shirking its obligation, as mandated by the Supreme Court, to turn over to the defense lawyers any exculpatory evidence in government files. Nothing at the hearing, however, unfolded as anyone might have expected. It was obvious even to untrained observers that neither General Flynn nor his counsel were prepared for it.

Judge Sullivan, whom Powell has called the "judicial hero" of *Licensed to Lie*, is most famous for having held the prosecution's feet to the fire in the case of Senator Ted Stevens, as discussed in Chapter 3. He recognized the government's failure to produce evidence favorable to the defense, dismissed the charges against Stevens, and excoriated the government for its misconduct. Indeed, Sullivan is one of the few federal judges who have been willing to hold the government to the high standards to which it should be held, given the Supreme Court's mandate that it seek "justice—not convictions."

Powell was shocked when it seemed a "different" Emmet G. Sullivan appeared on the bench that day. He began the hearing by noting that the government had just that morning, at 10:13, filed documents it had "inadvertently omitted" from its previous filings. Those were documents Judge Sullivan had ordered to be filed because the sentencing memo filed by the Flynn defense team noted the unusual ambush-interview of Flynn to distinguish his case from other prosecutions.

Even more shocking, in this high-profile case, and in a courtroom packed with media reporting it live, the almost unrecognizable Judge Sullivan got the facts of the case wrong. He effectively accused General Flynn of selling out his country while he was in the White House. No one knew where that came from—except perhaps the government, as one of the many things they can do is file information with the Court *ex parte* and under seal. Not even the defense knew everything the government had filed.

The judge cast the word "treason" around with abandon, causing the media to report for an hour that the judge was accusing Flynn of having committed this most heinous crime. Sullivan might as well have driven a wooden stake through the heart of a man descended from generations of military service to this country.

Judge Sullivan voiced his abject "disgust" for Flynn's conduct. He accused Flynn of working for the government of Turkey while he was in the White House. Aside from the fact that Turkey is one of America's strategic and NATO allies, Flynn had ended that brief contractual relationship before he accepted the position on President-Elect Trump's transition team, and he never worked *for* the government of Turkey. On advice of counsel, he had registered under FARA upon demand of the FARA section of the Department of Justice and stated that some of the work he did on a three-month project may have inured to the principal benefit of Turkey. However, his firm was not paid by Turkey but by a businessman.

Judge Sullivan returned after a recess and tried to clarify and retract his worst remarks, but the damage had already been done. He made clear that he intended to send Flynn to prison. After the recess, Flynn accepted the judge's offer to postpone his sentencing while he provided further cooperation to the government on its FARA-related case against Flynn's former business partner, Bijan Rafiekian, in the Eastern District of Virginia.

• • •

General Flynn's guilty plea epitomizes every problem with the plea process. Yes, Flynn entered a guilty plea, but that does not mean he did anything illegal. All it means is that he saw no other way out—like so many others standing in similar shoes, including a disproportionate number of young minority men who have no resources whatsoever. When the full might and weight of the federal government are brought to bear against an individual, many see no choice but to plead guilty to a lesser charge, even if it has been concocted by prosecutors. And prosecutors depend upon this natural reaction as a means to elicit a false answer, thus allowing them to put the kind of pressure on the target that gets him to "sing and compose." Now imagine that the pressure is applied with the immeasurable hubris and endless funding of the "special prosecutor" and his relentless and heavily armed team.

The beating a defendant takes with a guilty plea is less than the beating a defendant takes if he dares to fight, and finds himself in the real torture of solitary confinement, while his friends, family, and business associates are harassed, threatened, and indicted themselves. That is what happened to Paul Manafort (as described in Chapter 7). Prosecutions in Mueller's and Weissmann's prior inquisitions have extended for as long as ten years, a life-wrecking period of expensive and all-consuming trench warfare where one side has unlimited resources to engage in a war of attrition. Several defendants in Enron-related litigation pleaded guilty after obtaining verdicts of acquittals but having juries unable to reach a verdict or "hung" on some counts, which enabled the government to prosecute the defendants again, and so they faced their *third* trial. There is no limit to the number of times the government can drag a defendant through a trial when the jury does not return verdicts of "not guilty" on all counts.

Can you, the reader, even imagine what you would do if, despite being a law-abiding good citizen all your life, you suddenly found yourself the target of a "special counsel" investigation, threatened with life in prison, threatened with the indictment of your children and your business associates, your savings completely drained, having to start a Go-Fund-Me account, and interrogated for hour after hour by people dying to trap you and send you to prison?

Those who have not endured a criminal prosecution, or been close to someone who has, cannot begin to imagine the toll it takes on everyone involved—the entire family. The stress is incomprehensible. The world is upside down. It's the Twilight Zone. For someone who *has* experienced this system—whether as a target or as the lawyer for a target—it is difficult to deem this a "justice" system in any meaningful sense.

General Flynn's case exemplifies a second problem encountered, albeit not as often, in the plea process. The judge is not required to accept the prosecutor's sentencing recommendation. Sometimes this benefits the defendant—as prosecutors often want a greater sentence than is warranted—but in Flynn's case it did quite the opposite. The primary incentive in the prosecutor's toolkit for coercing a guilty plea is the power to offer a deal for less time in prison. If the judge doesn't accept that, it eliminates most of the prosecutor's leverage.

Flynn is now branded a traitor by some, grossly unfairly, because he didn't fight the charges—at least by the date of his originally scheduled sentencing.[†] Once a defendant has pleaded guilty, he is required to admit to—in effect, to adopt—what the government drafts as the "factual basis" for the plea. The government is often very liberal in what it includes in that factual basis.

One need only look at the example of the plea and factual basis to which President Trump's former lawyer Michael Cohen agreed. Cohen entered a plea of guilty to two counts of "election law violations" that are completely unprecedented. That is, as can happen in federal prosecutions, those two "election law violations" are not crimes. As in the Arthur Andersen and Merrill Lynch cases, the prosecutors made up these offenses, but Cohen stands convicted of five federal felonies. So, Cohen is not actually guilty of what Cohen pleaded guilty to, but the prosecution will try to get mileage out of

---

† Flynn's entire case took a dramatic turn when Powell undertook his representation in the summer of 2019 as he was cooperating in the Eastern District of Virginia. As of this writing, the case is still in progress, and the details of the turn-around will have to await Powell's next book.

that plea agreement to use against others. Michael Cohen will be dancing to the federal prosecutors' tune like a trained monkey until they, who hold the leash and play the tune, say otherwise. Indeed, he was sent to prison even after extensive cooperation, and then the prosecutors are able to dangle over his head the possibility of a sentence reduction if he proves more "cooperative" after he has spent some time "in the system."[10]

The third problem with the guilty plea process is that the better the deal the prosecutors offer a truly guilty defendant, the more that defendant must "cooperate" with the government to its satisfaction—which is determined solely at the discretion of the prosecutors. They can require thousands of hours of interviews, and testimony in multiple trials, and can postpone the cooperator's sentencing until they have squeezed everything they want out of him. A judge will often postpone imposing sentence until after the prosecutor has certified to the judge that the defendant has in fact "cooperated." Thus, the defendant dances to the prosecutor's tune to earn his reduced sentence. It is the extraordinary person who has the integrity to resist a prosecutor's efforts to put words in his mouth that provide "evidence" to support the prosecutor's "narrative" or "theory" of the case.

Once a defendant has signed a plea-and-cooperation deal, he has indeed sold his soul to the devil. At least two cooperating defendants in the authors' personal experience have spent time in solitary confinement—the prosecutors' way of persuading them to "cooperate" more fully.[11] Solitary confinement is total sensory deprivation. It is a means of torture, and often can drive a sane man insane within twenty-four hours. People will agree to anything to get out of solitary confinement, and it is the rare person who can endure this kind of torture without capitulating to the prosecutors' demands. Testimony produced by such a system is virtually guaranteed to be false.

It happened to Ted Stevens when he was a United States senator, as both authors discussed in our prior books (Powell in *Licensed to Lie* and Silverglate in *Three Felonies a Day*). It happened to the many people later exonerated by the Innocence Project, and to the many whose names fill the National Registry of Exonerations.[12] It is happening in front of our eyes.

There are innocent people in our prisons right now—many on guilty pleas. Selective political persecutions of people who have been targeted, with concocted crimes, is contrary to everything the Department of Justice is supposed to represent. It is imperative that we not send another innocent person to prison.

• • •

The first step in reforming the plea process is to compel prosecutors to produce all material required by the *Brady* rule before a defendant can be asked to plead. Some courts require this, but others do not. No one should enter a plea of guilty until he possesses any evidence the government has that might exonerate him or defeat the government's case.

Second, as we discuss in Chapter 7, there should be a limit on the number of charges that prosecutors can bring in nonviolent, first-offender, non-drug cases, and perhaps in all cases except when there are specific, direct victims of the defendants' alleged crimes. If the prosecutors cannot pile on insurmountable charges, defendants will stand a chance of mounting a defense even through a trial. Trials will be shorter, there can be more trials (and fewer plea bargains), and the system should be fairer overall. That alone will improve the fairness of the plea process.

Third, there should be no toll imposed upon a defendant for defending himself. The right to trial by jury is protected by the Constitution, and no one should be penalized for exercising that right.[13] As it stands now, judges often "charge rent on the courtroom," in that the sentence will be longer for anyone who goes to trial simply because he went to trial. The sentencing guidelines provide for an obstruction enhancement,[14] and while it isn't black-and-white, most pre-sentence officers and judges add two levels to the defendant's offense level if a defendant testifies and is convicted. The guidelines already provide for a two-level decrease for acceptance of responsibility, which is usually reserved only for those who plead guilty.[15] But a defendant should be able to testify in his own defense without incurring any penalty for it. Otherwise, we are penalizing him for exercising a constitutional right.

Fourth, the practice of prosecutors to offer targets or defendants a non-prosecution deal or a substantially lower sentence for "cooperation" in delivering testimony demanded of them should be abolished. The practice is clearly coercive to the point of producing whatever testimony the prosecutor seeks, rather than the truth. Just as a defense lawyer would be indicted for offering any incentive to a witness in exchange for testimony, so a prosecutor should not be able effectively to bribe or extort his witnesses. At the very least, someone like Andrew Fastow, the Enron CFO who actually stole millions of dollars and was guilty of more egregious offenses than anyone he testified against, should be required to serve a term of imprisonment at least half the term of anyone convicted as a result of his testimony.

Sadly, prosecutors send innocent people to prison every day— whether by guilty plea or wrongful conviction. Prosecutors withhold evidence of innocence, they destroy evidence, and they have absolute immunity—even for their intentional wrongdoing. They then dangle sentence reduction over the head of the incarcerated. When there were fewer prosecutors and substantially fewer laws, the problem was not as bad. Now the criminal code has exploded, and since the terrorist attack of 9-11, so have the numbers of federal prosecutors. The system is ripe for corruption from start to finish, at every stage. Those who appreciate the meaning and true import of the phrase "rule of law" understand that this system must change now.

The many doubters out there owe it to themselves and to the nation to educate themselves. Between the willingness of Congress to turn almost everything into a federal crime and the ability of federal prosecutors to stretch those statutes beyond imagination, there is no one in this country who could not be indicted if a prosecutor like Robert Mueller or Andrew Weissmann were to scour our life's records. We are all subject to this abusive prosecutorial system, which has no realistic checks or balances.

CHAPTER SIX

AN OFFER HE CAN'T REFUSE

Use Immunity Statutes—
Not Backroom Deals—to
Compel Testimony

Prosecutors have unlimited discretion to cut deals with the worst of the worst criminals to "persuade" them to testify against higher-ups whom the prosecutors have targeted for criminal prosecution. During the 2013 federal racketeering trial of James "Whitey" Bulger, former South Boston mob boss, jurors learned firsthand how federal prosecutors cut such deals in the high-profile trials that often make their careers. One of those jurors, Janet Uhlar, summed it up by noting simply, "It was a very disgusting feeling, actually, a dirty feeling."[1] After all, federal prosecutors had allowed murderers to trade testimony for their lives.

Bulger's hitman, John Martorano, could have faced the death penalty for any one of twenty counts of first-degree murder. Instead, as a government witness in 1999, he cut the sweetest deal of his life: fourteen years in prison, only twelve of which he actually served, in exchange for his testimony against his former boss. Martorano was released in 2007, and he repeated his sworn testimony against Bulger—which included his admitting to the jury in 2013 his own responsibility for twenty murders. Martorano admitted on the stand that a film company paid him $250,000 for the rights to his life story. He also received about $70,000 for his role in helping Howie Carr, a *Boston Herald* columnist, turn out *Hitman: The Untold Story of Johnny Martorano: Whitey Bulger's Enforcer and the Most Feared Gangster in the Underworld.*[2] Perhaps most shocking of all, the U.S. Drug Enforcement Agency paid him $20,000 in "gate money" upon his release from prison.[3]

Bulger's former henchman Stephen "The Rifleman" Flemmi was another "turned" witness for the government. Flemmi had pleaded guilty in 2003 to racketeering charges, including ten murders in Florida and Oklahoma, and was sentenced to life imprisonment. In the plea agreement, prosecutors took the death penalty off the table as long as Flemmi "cooperate[d] fully with law enforcement agents and government attorneys...at any hearing and trial,"[4] including, of course, Bulger's. Flemmi's plea specifies that "Defendant's failure to *continue* to cooperate...after sentence is imposed shall constitute a breach of this Agreement by Defendant" (emphasis added).[5] In other words, Flemmi must "sing" for his life, and if prosecutors don't like the aria they hear, they can revoke his plea agreement at any time. As Professor Alan Dershowitz has often said, given the pressure on cooperating witnesses to please the prosecutors, they often "compose" rather than merely sing.

The life-or-death deals that prosecutors made with Flemmi and Martorano left some jurors unsure whether Bulger or the witness blaming him had committed certain murders. Bulger was ultimately found guilty of 31 out of the 32 counts against him, including eleven gruesome murders. His conviction likely resulted in part from the damning testimony his former colleagues provided. But exactly how reliable was this information? After all, Martorano and other turned witnesses like Flemmi had the strongest incentive possible to appease the prosecution—even if that meant lying to the jury. And furthermore, is this truly the price we want to pay to put away one criminal, even one as bad as Bulger? Do we really have to—should we—absolve one murderer to get another? And when we do so, are we doing irreparable damage to the credibility of the criminal justice system?

Bulger was, admittedly, an unsympathetic character. But this method of using what is essentially bought testimony to secure convictions is endemic to the criminal justice system.† We must also question whether that good a deal is even necessary. More often than they should, these coerced witnesses help put innocent people behind bars (or in the gas chamber).[6] How is this not bribery? Would it not be a criminal offense were the defendant to try to encourage a witness to testify for him in the same way? To take one example, Paul Manafort faced additional criminal charges simply for attempting to contact a witness for his defense.

What's astonishing is that federal prosecutors don't *need* to make these kinds of backroom deals—ones that put the likes of John Martorano back on the street and incentivize perjury—to obtain co-conspirator testimony.[7] Longstanding immunity statutes can be used to compel testimony from individuals who might otherwise claim their Fifth Amendment right to remain silent.

Developments in federal statutory law and attendant prosecutorial practices have resulted in a perverse system of witness bribery that is available only to the prosecution. Closing loopholes in the federal sentencing guidelines and returning to the traditional use of immunity statutes to compel testimony would help correct the problem. The tools used to compel testimony should be employed *prior* to the testimony, with post-testimony *penalties* for perjury rather than *rewards* afterward for the testimony that prosecutors wanted to hear. This is essential, lest the government offer unconscionably sweet deals to convicted felons, consummated *after* the desired testimony is delivered, and thereby continue to incentivize perjured testimony.

• • •

---

† Harvey Silverglate has seen this tactic used in many cases throughout his career.

The use of informants is not a new phenomenon in criminal law. In certain cases, the testimony of an "inside man" is crucial to cracking a case. The great Judge Learned Hand wrote that in cases of conspiracy, "it is usually necessary to rely on [informants] or upon accomplices because the criminals will almost certainly proceed covertly."[8]

But in recent decades the use of informants in the federal criminal justice system has become toxic, and it has been abused by unscrupulous prosecutors willing to do anything to win convictions. As evidenced by the Bulger trial, the current system puts enormous pressure on potential witnesses to testify according to what will be most helpful to the government, rather than to simply tell the truth. With prosecutors holding the power to determine just how "cooperative" a witness is, and in turn to petition the court for the reduction of a sentence, a witness knows that he will be rewarded only if his testimony jibes with the prosecution's "theories" and needs, and results in more convictions.

Moreover, prosecutions under vague criminal statutes such as conspiracy,[9] aiding and abetting,[10] and mail and wire fraud (including "honest services" fraud),[11] often showcase ambiguous situations where a target's actions could easily be interpreted by a jury as perfectly normal and legitimate business, unless someone is present to testify that the target's intentions were fraudulent or otherwise unlawful. This situation allows prosecutors to use informants or "co-conspirators" to convict (or squeeze guilty pleas out of) the innocent and the guilty alike.

Most criminal defense lawyers would be hard-pressed to remember the last federal case they tried that did not rely heavily on a turned informant-witness who started working with the Department of Justice either before or after an indictment that initially was or could potentially have been directed against the informant. The primary reason the informant or cooperating co-conspirator occupies such a prominent place in current federal criminal law enforcement is a variety of Draconian sentencing practices enacted by Congress, known as "mandatory minimums."

In the second half of the twentieth century, Congress passed a wave of these mandatory minimum laws requiring that judges incarcerate convicted felons for decades.[12] It also created federal sentencing guidelines, a further culprit in the vast increase in federal sentences.[13] Judges were increasingly deprived of their historic discretion to impose sentences within a generally wide range of incarceration and nonincarceration alternatives, balancing such factors as the seriousness and nature of the crime, the defendant's remorse, supposedly relevant factors in the defendant's life, and society's perceived need for vengeance or deterrence.

Oddly, the creation of the sentencing guidelines was at first thought to be a clear sign of civilized and liberal progress in the criminal justice system, because it was aimed at eliminating favoritism that Congress suspected was rampant. In theory, the rich and powerful or the well-connected would now be treated just like everybody else, according to an objective checklist of aggravating and mitigating factors.[14] But in practice, the new system significantly jacked up sentences for the connected and nonconnected alike, and, crucially, it *transferred sentencing discretion from judges to prosecutors.*

This transfer of power was exacerbated by the creation of an escape hatch from the severe sentences. The rules in the United States Code, specifically 18 U.S.C. § 3553(e), allow judges to sentence below the guidelines range, or even below the statutory mandatory minimum sentence where such a mandatory sentence is applicable, only when the prosecutor has filed a motion asserting that the defendant provided "substantial assistance" to investigators and prosecutors in the investigation and conviction of another prosecutorial target.[15] While this enables the turned witness to escape a life in federal prison or even the death penalty, it also gives prosecutors excessive leverage to trade plea bargains for "valuable" testimony and gives vulnerable defendants a strong incentive to testify in accordance with the prosecution's theory of the case, even if that means they would have to perjure themselves.

In addition, a provision of the sentencing guidelines directs that a defendant who either pleads guilty or is convicted after a trial may escape the full impact of the suggested sentence if the prosecutor files with the court a document that has come to be known as a "5(K) motion," saying that the defendant "has provided substantial assistance in the investigation or prosecution of another person who has committed an offense."[16]

Section 3553(e) of the federal criminal code and the "5(K) motion" afford prosecutors undue power in sentencing. Both should be eliminated, to return power traditionally held by the judiciary back to judges. Mandatory minimum sentences should also be abolished for many offenses and greatly reduced for others, so that sentencing discretion is given back to judges rather than prosecutors.

Fully recognizing their extraordinary power, prosecutors aptly analogize this system to a departing passenger train. They will tell a target's lawyer that he should let his client know that "the train will soon be leaving the station," and that the client will either be onboard as a witness, or find himself abandoned to the role of defendant (or worse, "fall guy"). Every criminal defense lawyer who practices in the federal courts is fully aware of the "train leaving the station" moment when the client must decide whether to fight or switch sides. And switching sides disturbingly often means learning both to sing and to compose. The status of cooperating witness promises a shorter sentence (or, in a case of "extraordinary" cooperation, no sentence at all), while the status of defendant threatens the proverbial "boxcar" sentence.

This paradigm, where a defendant is wholly at the mercy of prosecutors, is not that much of a departure from the model for the military's and the Department of Justice's treatment of captured suspected terrorists in the "War on Terror" that commenced after the terrorist attacks of September 11, 2001. At the time, the Bush administration argued that it had the power to detain indefinitely anyone captured on the field of battle in the war against terrorism, by declaring such captives "enemy combatants." They could be tried by military tribunals, or just held indefinitely until the government declared the war against terrorism to be over. Carl Takei, now an ACLU attorney, argued as a law student at Boston College that indefinite detention provided a powerful incentive for any such captive, including one who might credibly argue for his total innocence, to engage in a plea bargain in the federal criminal justice system where a guilty plea and cooperation would produce a sentence of definite duration.[17]

Similarly, defendants facing harsh sentencing guidelines and mandatory minimum sentences cannot be trusted to provide reliable testimony when they know that their punishment will be reduced only by testimony helpful to the government. It should come as no surprise that witnesses under incomprehensible pressures will tailor their testimony to suit the needs, expectations, and too often the scripts (or, more politely, hints) conveyed by prosecutors. Sometimes, cooperating witnesses are interviewed by government agents and prosecutors so many times that they can no longer remember whether they themselves said or thought something or if it was said by the government agent or prosecutor.[18]

Moreover, the prosecutor will transmit his suggestions for cooperation to the putative cooperating witness's lawyer more often than to the witness himself. As a practical matter, this insulates the conversation from disclosure at a trial, because the witness's conversations with his lawyer are protected by the attorney-client privilege. A witness who has not spoken directly with the prosecutor on the subject does not have to disclose at trial the full extent of his expectations for how well he will be treated if he delivers a knockout blow against the defendant on trial. When a bargain like this is reached in a conversation between the prosecutor and a witness's attorney, it almost never gets disclosed to the defendant or his defense counsel. Thus, even though just about every participant in the system—often including the judge—realizes that such conversations have occurred and such promises have been made or strongly inferred, the scam proceeds with all parties averting their eyes.[19]

Other methods of witness coercion—made possible by the enormous discretion accorded to federal prosecutors—can be yet more nefarious. Prosecutors wield powerful threats: In one of Silverglate's cases, prosecutors threatened to indict his noncooperating client, the client's wife, his son, his sister, and his elderly father for conspiracy to evade payment of income taxes, on the theory that since these family members benefited from the client's alleged tax evasion, they were technically conspirators in the evasion scheme.[20] Such practices are unconscionable but happen regularly, as discussed in Chapter 5.

The technique of bribing (and even threatening) witnesses seems indistinguishable from extortion or obstruction of justice, and it would be criminal if done by a witness, defendant, or either's counsel. Nevertheless, it is standard operating procedure for prosecutors. Some courts have recognized this as a problem. On several occasions, federal courts have tried to curb or even eliminate the practice of offering prospective witnesses inducements to obtain their testimony against other targets.

Perhaps the most prominent effort by a federal court to do away with the practice of rewarding prosecution witnesses occurred in the case of *United States v. Singleton*, when in 1998 a federal district judge and a three-judge panel of the U.S. Court of Appeals for the Tenth Circuit declared the practice of coercing or rewarding witnesses to be in obvious and literal violation of the federal witness bribery statute.[21] But when the Department of Justice assured the court—erroneously, in our opinion—that it could not successfully do its job without engaging in such practices, the full bench of that circuit unceremoniously, and without apparent shame, reversed the panel.[22]

In an earlier case in the Eighth Circuit, *United States v. Waterman*, the trial judge refused to exclude the rewarded witness's testimony, and a three-judge panel of the circuit voted to reverse and exclude the coerced testimony, only to have the full membership of the circuit reconsider the issue and split down the middle. The split had the practical effect of affirming the trial judge's approval of the tactic.[23]

And the same issue—the legality of rewarded witness testimony, particularly where the witness stands to receive his reward only if he gets the jury to convict—came up in the First Circuit in a drug prosecution. The trial judge threw out the testimony, but the court of appeals dutifully sustained the practice.[24] Thus, despite the obvious discomfort that some courts have had with these practices of rewarding or coercing witnesses, and despite an occasional rebellion from a few particularly principled trial or appellate judges, the practice remains firmly entrenched and unsupervised.

Were Congress to eliminate the practice of rewarding cooperating witnesses for their testimony, it would hardly mean that such testimony would be unavailable. Indeed, federal statutes contain adequate provisions for *compelling* (rather than *bribing*) witnesses to provide *truthful* testimony. Because the Fifth Amendment to the Constitution protects a person from being "compelled in any criminal case to be a witness against himself," as the witness necessarily would do were he to testify that he and the target committed the crime together, Congress over the years has enacted so-called witness "immunity" statutes to remove the risk of self-incrimination from testifying. These statutes provide that prosecutors may obtain court orders commanding a witness to testify at either a grand jury proceeding or a trial against a defendant. If the witness refuses to testify and instead invokes his privilege against self-incrimination, a court may order that the witness's testimony or any information derived from that testimony may not be used against him (so-called "use plus fruits" immunity). A witness who refuses to testify after being granted immunity may be held in contempt and incarcerated indefinitely until he changes his mind.[25]

This system eliminates the incentive for witnesses to lie, because the witness compelled by the threat of contempt and protected by immunity has nothing to gain from the prosecutor that depends on the *content* of his testimony. But prosecutors do not like, and hence rarely use, the formal witness immunity statutes, because the testimony comes *after* the immunity is imposed, and so the prosecutor loses considerable control over what the witness says. Under this formal statutory immunity system, the prosecutor can punish the witness for his testimony only if the prosecutor can prove, after the testimony has been given, that the witness has lied. Under this long-established but rarely used witness immunity system, the prosecution does not get to write the witness's script.

Granting "use" immunity to witnesses whose testimony prosecutors deem necessary to the conviction of a co-conspirator (or any defendant, for that matter) is a more ethical—and viable—alternative to the current system of veritable witness bribery.

Additionally, Congress should strike from the U.S. criminal code 18 U.S.C. § 3553(e), the statute that allows judges to sentence below the guidelines in the event a defendant provides "substantial assistance" to the government, and it should eliminate the "5(k) motion" loophole in the sentencing guidelines that prescribes the same tactic. These rather simple measures would go a long way toward ensuring that federal criminal trials serve *justice* rather than the desires and personal interests of turned witnesses and careerist prosecutors. In addition, the person who actually committed the crime should receive substantially the same sentence as the person he testifies against—who often played a far less significant role but was the witness's superior and therefore a "high-value target" to the prosecutors seeking to notch their belts with high-profile convictions.

CHAPTER SEVEN

PROSECUTORIAL MISCONDUCT

Who Will Prosecute the Prosecutor?

I t happens more often than anyone wants to admit. Countless people have spent decades in state and federal prisons wrongly convicted of crimes because of deliberate misconduct by prosecutors—none of whom have been held accountable for their wrongdoing.[1] To say that we find this an outrage is an understatement. How can any of us call it justice? How will the system ever improve if prosecutors who commit what amounts to obstruction of justice, perjury, or subornation of perjury are allowed not only to escape scot-free, but to prosper and be promoted because of their crimes? And then to obtain lucrative jobs in the private sector or the most senior positions in government?

Prosecutorial misconduct comes in many forms. The crux of the problem is that prosecutors—whether state or federal—have extremely broad discretion, and virtually no supervision. On top of that, they enjoy absolute immunity from lawsuits even for deliberate wrongdoing. Judges are loath to reverse criminal convictions, at the risk of freeing a real criminal because of something a prosecutor did wrong, and bar associations rarely take any action to police prosecutorial misconduct.

On the federal side, the Department of Justice, through its Office of Professional Responsibility (OPR), seems intent on circling the wagons to protect prosecutors from any repercussions even for their deliberate wrongdoing, at least in the past fifteen years or so. Sometime in the Bush administration, OPR stopped releasing the names of prosecutors who had committed misconduct, and the new practice solidified during the opaque Obama administration.[2]

One of the most egregious forms of prosecutorial misconduct is suppressing or hiding evidence favorable to the defense, in violation of the *Brady* doctrine. As we noted in Chapter 3, the obligation of prosecutors to disclose such evidence to defense counsel arose from a United States Supreme Court decision in 1963, *Brady v. Maryland*, and has since become accepted law in the federal justice system and in every state. But the *Brady* doctrine is frequently violated in practice, as in the case of Ted Stevens, the former United States senator, and in the case of Bernard Baran, the Massachusetts daycare worker. Many more violations, of course, are never discovered.

Prosecutorial misconduct comes in many other forms as well. Prosecutors have unlimited discretion in what kinds of offenses to charge and how many, as Robert H. Jackson, the attorney general, pointed out in his speech to United States attorneys in 1940.[3] They can "stack" so many charges against anyone that one act of misconduct can result in charges that could imprison someone for the rest of his life.

Prosecutors have unbridled discretion in how and when to obtain and execute search warrants and arrests. We've seen any number of instances of strong-arm tactics in the 2017–2019 investigation of Russian interference in the 2016 presidential election and related matters. Some well-known private citizens endured the trauma of predawn raids by heavily armed SWAT teams, while others were permitted to appear with counsel at a scheduled time. It's all up to the prosecutor.

Prosecutors routinely threaten to indict not only the defendant and/or witnesses but also members of the target's family. Sometimes these threats are empty, but who can afford the gamble? A prosecutor can indict "a ham sandwich," as we have illustrated. So threats to indict family members are painfully effective in inducing unfounded guilty pleas or cooperation agreements that produce less than accurate testimony. Something needs to be done to stop these threats, which would amount to extortion were they made by anyone other than a prosecutor.

Another outrageous prosecutorial abuse is what we call targeting. It is reminiscent of Joseph Stalin's chief of secret police, Lavrentiy Beria, who said: "Show me the man, and I will find you the crime." Even in America, a crime can be found to pin on anyone, as then Attorney General Jackson observed. There is no precise defense for this in our law. It's not supposed to happen. The closest existing legal defense would seem to be what is called "selective prosecution," but the law defines it more narrowly now, in a way that does not include targeting for political or personal reasons.[4]

We all watched as the special counsel chose to prosecute Republicans with any relationship to President Trump for false-statement offenses or others that have also been committed by countless Democrats, who either have been given outright immunity or their crimes have been ignored. The American public sees this, and people are outraged.

Congress has also contributed to the problem. It has created so many crimes that prosecutors can find multiple offenses to apply to the same conduct and something to pin on anyone. This pushes us ever closer to being a police state—a place where an ordinary person might commit three felonies in a typical day without knowing it, as Harvey Silverglate demonstrated in his previous book. Add in the outrageous number of federal regulations[5] that creative prosecutors turn into federal crimes as part of a conspiracy or through the aiding-and-abetting statute, and the number of possibilities for criminal violations extends "to infinity and beyond."[6]

How can the public have any respect for something called a system of justice that tolerates such abuses and does not apply the law equally? The rule of law—meaning its equal application to all Americans regardless of political party, social standing, or any other subjective factor—is a bedrock principle of our Republic. This chapter will address several distinct problems and propose solutions for them: 1) stacking charges; 2) strong-arm arrests and searches; 3) threatening defendants or witnesses and family members; 4) selective prosecution; and 5) overcriminalization. These practices are antithetical to our Constitution and our foundational legal principles.

1. STACKING CHARGES

Back in the old days, when Sidney Powell was an assistant United States attorney, we taught our young prosecutors to choose their best four or five counts against most defendants, even those against whom we could level many serious charges. We followed this practice in most cases—except those so egregious or involving so many victims that multiple counts were required to acknowledge the effect on the victims themselves and the community writ large.

We did so for many reasons. Four or five felony counts, in most cases, presents the prospect of twenty to twenty-five years in prison, as most federal felonies carry a possible term of imprisonment of at least five years. Many carry a possible term of imprisonment of substantially more than that. With the enactment of so many drug offenses carrying mandatory minimum terms of imprisonment, it's even worse.

An indictment limited to four to five counts outlines a case that can usually be tried within a week, and it is much easier for a jury to understand than a sprawling extravaganza. If the charges are solid—and they should be completely just and strong or the case should not be indicted—the jury will likely return a guilty verdict on all counts. The deck is stacked in favor of the government in all regards.

Apparently, that wasn't sufficient for a new breed of win-at-all-costs prosecutors, who instead of drafting reasonable indictments began piling on as many charges as they could. We're not sure when or why things changed—whether it was with the advent of federal sentencing guidelines, which gave prosecutors far too much power in their charging decisions, or with prosecutors' realization that the more convictions they chalked up, the higher they moved up the ladder. Or perhaps the press promoted the trend by giving sensational news coverage and headlines to huge cases with multicount indictments. We, the authors, can only tell you that it wasn't always this way. Powell worked for *nine* United States attorneys, from both political parties, and not one ever gave her any indication that her win-loss record mattered at all. They only told her to do it right, to make sure that a defendant was guilty before indicting him, and to seek justice—not convictions. The government wins more than 95 percent of its cases anyway. Piling on additional charges only crushes the defendant, exacerbates costs on both sides, and makes it impossible to defend. In the vast majority of cases, it serves no valid purpose.

Sometime in the last twenty years, the Department of Justice lost its way, and it has gone increasingly astray from seeking only justice. It must be turned around with all deliberate speed. Far too many injustices have been done. The DOJ has lost the respect and trust of the public, and it has become an international embarrassment instead of an icon.

Prosecutors have become very clever in creating charges to stack into an indictment. Indeed, in the cases of Arthur Andersen LLP and Enron Nigerian Barge (discussed at length in *Licensed to Lie*), prosecutors made up charges against Arthur Andersen in connection with its audit of the scandal-ridden Enron Corporation by piecing together parts of two different statutes. Arthur Andersen, which represented 2,500 publicly traded companies, was destroyed as soon as the government unsealed the indictment in 2002.[7] It was convicted in Houston by a jury fueled by public outrage from the fall of Enron—for which the prosecutors blamed Arthur Andersen. Two years later, however, the Supreme Court reversed the case in its entirety.[8]

Following quickly upon their success in annihilating Andersen and its 85,000 jobs, the prosecutors made up charges against four Merrill Lynch executives—criminalizing conduct that was a legal business transaction. The federal judge denied the valid motions to dismiss the indictment. Instead, he deferred to the prosecutors on virtually every argument and ruled in their favor at every turn.

Even though the indictment criminalized innocent conduct, and the prosecution was completely unprecedented, the Merrill executives were convicted and they served up to a year in prison while the Fifth Circuit considered their appeals. Finally, after oral arguments, the court reversed the concocted counts[†]—which again had pieced together statutes to make a new crime—but incalculable damage had been done by that time. One of the Merrill defendants had served eight months in a maximum-security federal transfer facility with the worst of the worst criminals in the federal system. The circuit court acquitted him on all charges.

It's happening all over again. Judge Dabney Friedrich, the wife of Matthew Friedrich, former Enron Task Force prosecutor—and one of the villains of *Licensed to Lie*—presided over Robert Mueller's indictment of the "Russian troll farm" that supposedly interfered in the 2016 election. Judge Friedrich recognized the special counsel's charges as "unprecedented," yet she refused to dismiss the indictment.[9]

That alone is an outrage. It is imperative that federal judges shake off their years as prosecutors, or their inherent bias in favor of the government, and step up to stop the abuses of the legal system by current federal prosecutors. Like countless federal judges before her—including Judge Melinda Harmon (who presided over

---

† Only two counts of the indictment against one of the four Merrill defendants were left standing after the appeals, and those should have been reversed. For the full explanation of that egregious injustice, see Powell, *Licensed to Lie.*

the Arthur Andersen case) and Judge Ewing Werlein (the Merrill Lynch case) in Houston—Judge Friedrich abdicated her responsibility to dismiss bogus charges brought by prosecutors who grossly overstepped their bounds.

The "unprecedented" nature of the charges brought before Judge Friedrich was apparent on the face of the indictments. There was literally no precedent case from any court anywhere in the country that supported such charges—nor did the statutes pursuant to which they were brought. Prosecutors are not permitted to pick parts of different statutes that they like and piece them together to define a new crime. It is unconstitutional, in violation of the doctrine of providing fair warning.[10] Moreover, only the legislative branch is empowered to create new crimes. Judges know this, and they should dismiss overreaching and overly creative indictments.

Abusive prosecutors have adopted the tactic of crushing a defendant under the weight of an indictment that no one can afford to defend.[11] For example, take the case of Jeffrey Skilling and Kenneth Lay, the two most senior executives at Enron. Most people don't realize that neither man stole a dime from Enron. Regardless of their business judgment, both men loved the company—as the prosecutors admitted in their closing arguments. They too lost everything along with the company. Skilling even offered to put $50 million of his money into the company to try to save it.

Enron Task Force prosecutors John Hueston, Sean Berkowitz, and Kathryn Ruemmler indicted and tried Lay and Skilling on more than a hundred counts, alleging complex financial transactions that neither the government nor the jury understood.[12] The case was effectively impossible to defend. The trial took sixteen weeks. Skilling's defense alone cost $100 million. And, of course, he and Lay were convicted. Everyone knew they would be from the beginning.

There was no way the Enron defendants could emerge from under a 110-count indictment in front of a Houston jury that had been inflamed with outrage for years by the time of the trial. The collapse of Enron devastated most of Houston and countless people across the country, and the Houston environment was so polluted with incessant adverse publicity that people literally talked about publicly lynching Lay and Skilling.[13]

More recently, consider Robert Mueller's prosecution of Paul Manafort, who briefly served as campaign manager for candidate Donald Trump in the 2016 election. Andrew Weissmann, the main villain of *Licensed to Lie*, and his boss, Mueller, targeted Manafort early on.[14] Indeed, Weissmann had Manafort in his sights before the special counsel operation officially began. Even though the Department of Justice had investigated Manafort in 2014 and did not charge him with any violations, Mueller and his fervent team poured through years of Manafort's financial records until they predictably pieced together a twelve-count indictment charging him with assorted tax and "money-laundering" violations. Despite his cooperation with the investigation, they executed a predawn search warrant on his home, agents searched his wife at gunpoint in their bed, and they arrested him and paraded him out of his home in front of a CNN camera crew that just happened to be ready and waiting at four in the morning.

Not satisfied with convicting Manafort on eight of the eighteen counts they ultimately brought against him in a hotly contested trial in the Eastern District of Virginia, the Office of Special Counsel brought additional charges against him in the District of Columbia, in front of a judge more favorable to the government's tactics.

In addition to the D.C. indictment alleging seven counts of money laundering, making false statements, and failing to register as a lobbyist, prosecutors returned to add charges of witness tampering and conspiracy because Manafort attempted to contact a witness that he hoped would testify for him. Prosecutors had not informed Manafort that the person was a government witness, and Manafort did not even have a conversation with the man. The witness-tampering "offense" was based on unreturned text messages.[15] Nonetheless, a federal judge in Washington, D.C., Amy Berman Jackson, promptly remanded Manafort to custody—prior to any of his trials—and he was placed in solitary confinement.[16] This significantly hindered his ability to work with his legal counsel on building his defense, and placing him in solitary was unconscionable.

What's the solution to all this piling on? It's simple. Stop it. The attorney general could institute a policy, immediately, that limits indictments to five to ten counts in most cases and fifteen counts in the more egregious cases, unless there are direct victims of separate offenses that must be vindicated.[†] This would go a long way toward leveling the playing field for defendants to have a chance to present a defense and to have a trial instead of being forced to plead guilty.

Unfortunately, we cannot rely on a mere DOJ policy, if adopted by the current administration, to withstand any action by subsequent administrations. It is imperative that Congress pass legislation, perhaps as part of a broader criminal justice reform package, that includes a limitation on the number of charges the government can bring against a defendant in all but the most egregious cases with direct and identifiable victims.[‡] Moreover, it's difficult to imagine circumstances in which a defendant should be forced to defend in multiple districts—as were Paul Manafort and untold others. There is nothing "just" about all this piling on. The right to trial by jury, a treasured provision of our Constitution, is protected only if people can afford to go to trial.

2. STRONG-ARM ARRESTS AND SEARCHES

Strong-arm arrests are often designed to intimidate and humiliate the target and to feed the prosecution's narrative to the press. The

---

† Of course, where there are actual direct victims of violence, fraud, drugs, or other clear crimes, and certainly including acts of terrorism, indictments should reflect the charges necessary to hold a defendant accountable for each actual victim.

‡ For example, in the horrific terrorist attack in New York in which a man drove a pickup truck down a sidewalk, killed eight people, and severely injured eleven others, justice demands there should be a count for every person injured.

arrest raids and searches on Paul Manafort and Roger Stone provide glaring examples of this abuse. Regardless of one's opinion of either person and one's political leanings, the predawn raids on them in their homes in front of waiting camera crews were inappropriate. The FBI and other law enforcement agencies reserve those tactics for drug cases and when they legitimately fear risk of violence or immediate destruction of evidence. Former leading FBI agents were appalled by these abuses of power.

Both Manafort and Stone were represented by counsel and had been cooperating in the special counsel investigation. They had produced documents, and neither had ever had any prior criminal encounter with "the system." Both were well-known businessmen with families, friends, colleagues, and significant ties to the community. Neither posed a flight risk.

Yet Manafort and Stone—courtesy of Robert Mueller and his lieutenant, Andrew Weissmann—were treated like international terrorists who are known to have explosive devices on their property and a massive weapons cache. Heavily armed agents awakened Manafort in his bed at gunpoint in a predawn raid of his house, even searching his nightgown-clad wife as if she might have a weapon. Can one even imagine enduring such terror and humiliation?

Much the same treatment was dealt to Roger Stone, longtime friend of Donald Trump. The colorful Mr. Stone had long been in the special counsel's crosshairs—as had many of the president's associates. Stone had also testified and cooperated with the investigation, was represented by counsel, and surely would have turned himself in, had he been asked. Instead, during a government shutdown when the FBI director, Christopher Wray, was complaining about scarce resources and his agents not being paid,[17] Mueller's office staged a predawn assault on Stone's residence—complete with a helicopter hovering above and frogmen in the canal behind the house. Prosecutors sent seventeen cars, a boat, and twenty-nine heavily armed agents to the home of a sixty-six-year old man who was neither a threat to anyone nor a flight risk—and they staged it all for CNN.[18]

We can't help but note the grossly disparate treatment the Department of Justice and the FBI accorded to Hillary Clinton and her team. Clinton was scheduled to have a conversation with the FBI at her convenience, surrounded by her co-conspirators, who were also lawyers. The government gave immunity to five of her colleagues, including two who had destroyed evidence on her computer. The FBI and the DOJ knew that Clinton's personal lawyer had her emails in a safe in his office. Those emails contained classified information, unlawfully in his possession—yet no raid was conducted on that lawyer's firm, as it was on President Trump's lawyer Michael Cohen.

Both the selective, disparate treatment and the strong-arm prosecutorial tactics reserved for the political opposition are abusive, repulsive, expensive, and unnecessary. We have watched in horror as they are used discriminatorily by prosecutors like Mueller and Weissmann to inflict as much fear, humiliation, and degradation on their targets as possible.

There was no legitimate reason for either raid, nor for the arrest of Roger Stone or of Paul Manafort to have been conducted as each was.[†] These tactics might be necessary for dangerous criminals such as organized crime figures, drug dealers, and suspected terrorists. But there is no place in a civilized society to use them against nonviolent people with no criminal record who are going to be released on personal recognizance bonds, are represented by counsel, have been cooperating in an investigation, and would surely report to court when asked. The treatment of Stone and Manafort is the stuff of which a police state is made.

The attorney general should immediately prohibit such tactics by any prosecutor and FBI office in the absence of probable cause to

---

† Federal magistrate judges had to sign off on those warrants, and the Stone indictment and raid appears to have been rushed to completion before the new attorney general, William Barr, took office. The judge should have stopped it.

believe the defendant is a danger to the community or a serious risk of flight. Congressional legislation or amendments to the Federal Rules of Criminal Procedure should follow.

3. COERCING PLEAS BY THREAT OF INDICTING FAMILY MEMBERS

Certainly, there are some cases where family members are truly co-conspirators and share equally with the primary defendant in the criminal scheme, but those cases are not the norm. Unfortunately, it has become routine among overzealous prosecutors to threaten to indict a family member if a target does not plead guilty or cooperate as demanded. Mueller's lieutenant Andrew Weissmann perfected this tactic in the Enron litigation, and countless prosecutors have used it to extort guilty pleas—even from innocent people—and cooperation agreements that meant saying whatever the prosecutor wanted the person to say.

In the Enron case, as mentioned earlier, Weissmann threatened to indict Andrew Fastow's wife, Lea, if he did not plead and cooperate. The couple had two small children. How much she actually knew about any of Fastow's shenanigans is dubious, but when Fastow failed to cooperate on Weissmann's deadline, the prosecutor made good on this threat. He indicted Lea Fastow on tax charges. She went to prison. Weissmann magnanimously allowed them to serve their sentences at different times so that the children had one parent at home. All it takes is one instructive example like that to make other targets fall in line. Weissmann and many other prosecutors have found the tactic especially effective when the threat to indict is focused on a child of the target.

That was one of the tactics used by Weissmann's special counsel team, including Brandon Van Grack and Zainab Ahmad, to extort a guilty plea from President Trump's national security advisor Michael Flynn.[19]

4. SELECTIVE PROSECUTION

Prosecutors have sole discretion as to whom to charge and for what offenses. For example, countless lawyers and lobbyists in Washington, D.C., are in violation of the Foreign Agent Registration Act every day. FARA requires anyone working on behalf of a foreign government to register with the Department of Justice.[20] Those violations have been handled civilly and gone unprosecuted for decades, but Robert Mueller resurrected FARA from oblivion to charge people connected with Donald Trump. Even worse, he indicted Tony Podesta, a prominent Democrat and brother of Hillary Clinton's campaign chairman, along with Paul Manafort, but gave Podesta immunity from prosecution.[21] This reeks of unfairness, a double standard, and is impossible to justify to the already disillusioned public that readily recognizes these abuses.

We have witnessed the same discriminatory enforcement of the statute that prohibits lying to federal agents. The Office of Special Counsel has used the statute to prosecute and squeeze associates of President Trump, while countless Democrats and others, including James Comey, James Clapper, Andrew McCabe, and Hillary Clinton, have lied to Congress, courts, or the FBI, yet no charges have been brought against them. The American people see this double standard.

For the rule of law to mean something, the law must be applied equally without regard to political party, status, or power. Abuse of power should concern everyone regardless of political affiliation. Anyone can be impermissibly targeted without probable cause and selectively prosecuted if these abuses are not corrected. Deciding who and what to charge falls within the extremely broad and unsupervised discretion of the federal prosecutor. It has become increasingly apparent that the rule of law requires some guidelines to be set.

Congressman Matt Gaetz of Florida saw this precise problem

and recently introduced the Justice for All Act.[22] The gist of Gaetz's proposed legislation is that if prosecutors are going to prosecute one person for lying to Congress, they should prosecute all persons who have done so. That is only fair, and one would think it does not have to be legislated, but apparently it does.

There is a legal defense called "selective prosecution." The Supreme Court stated in *Yick Wo v. Hopkins* (1886):

> Though the law itself be fair on its face, and impartial in appearance, yet, if it is applied and administered by public authority with an evil eye and an unequal hand, so as practically to make unjust and illegal discriminations between persons in similar circumstances, material to their rights, the denial of equal justice is still within the prohibition of the constitution."[23]

The application of this defense has been extremely limited, however. In actual practice in criminal prosecutions, as long as the government has probable cause to believe a crime has been committed, there is a presumption that it has acted in good faith, and the prosecutor has broad discretion.[24] This allows prosecutors to pick and choose whom they want to prosecute—far too much discretion in our hyperpoliticized environment, which includes documented abuses.

The presumption that the prosecution has acted in good faith is no longer valid. At a minimum, it must be rebuttable with clear and convincing evidence of bad faith, targeting, or disparate treatment. In addition, there must be a review process within the Department of Justice and each of the United States Attorneys' Offices to address the equal application of the law to similarly situated persons known to have committed the same offenses. Also, it would be far more equitable for the Department of Justice to issue a formal notice that it is going to begin enforcing FARA violations (or other arcane or unheard-of federal statutes) by the criminal prosecution of anyone who did not register within thirty days, rather than single out individuals to charge for leverage to squeeze for information in the special counsel investigation. All known violations should be prosecuted on a consistent basis—or all should be handled civilly, as they had been previously. Statutes that have more of a regulatory focus should be handled by fines. It is difficult to imagine a registration violation that warrants a federal prosecution and prison time.

In his famous speech on the responsibilities of a federal prosecutor, Robert H. Jackson remarked:

> The prosecutor has more control over life, liberty, and reputation than any other person in America. His discretion is tremendous.
>
> He can have citizens investigated and, if he is that kind of person, he can have this done to the tune of public statements and veiled or unveiled intimations. Or the prosecutor may choose a more subtle course and simply have a citizen's friends interviewed. The prosecutor can order arrests, present cases to the grand jury in secret session, and on the basis of his one-sided presentation of the facts, can cause the citizen to be indicted and held for trial.
>
> He may dismiss the case before trial, in which case the defense never has a chance to be heard. Or he may go on with a public trial.

Defense counsel, especially in these targeted prosecutions, should much more vigorously argue selective prosecution, and courts should be far more cognizant of this issue and give more teeth to this defense. There are cases and language available to use.[25] Legislation could also be enacted to bolster this defense or to offset or eliminate the presumption of good faith the prosecution enjoys with no limits. At a minimum, upon a showing by clear and convincing evidence, a defendant should be allowed to defend himself as having been singled out for some wrongful purpose while others like him have been given a pass for the same conduct, and courts should dismiss counts upon the requisite showing of targeting or disparate treatment.

5. OVERCRIMINALIZATION

Congress has passed too many criminal laws, many of which are overlapping and others far too broad. On top of this, overly creative prosecutors have learned to expand existing statutes beyond recognition by combining parts of different statutes to make up new crimes—a practice well documented in *Licensed to Lie*. Prosecutors also take the broad conspiracy and aiding-and-abetting statutes and incorporate into them federal regulations that were never intended to be criminal offenses.

Prosecutors have used the overly broad wire and mail fraud statutes, and the vague "honest services" statute, to criminalize innocent business conduct. In *United States v. Brown*, four Merrill Lynch executives each spent up to a year in prison on the government's theory that they had violated the "honest services" wire fraud statute—even though they were just doing their jobs.[26] The Fifth Circuit reversed the conspiracy and wire fraud convictions against all the Merrill defendants, but they had been denied bail pending appeal, and irreparable damage was done. One defendant was completely acquitted—after he had served eight months in a maximum-security federal transfer facility alongside the most dangerous criminals.[27] These kinds of abuses of the law must be prevented. There is no adequate remedy after the fact.

We need a Walmart-size rollback of federal regulations and vague or duplicitous federal criminal statutes. Until then, the most innocent among us are at risk of committing multiple daily crimes and being targeted by crafty prosecutors.

◆   ◆   ◆

The solutions for these problems rest primarily with Congress. Accomplishing reform will present difficult political challenges, but here are some recommendations.

1. Congress should pass a simple bill providing that only Congress can create a criminal offense. This legislation should make clear that nothing in the massive and impenetrable Code of Federal Regulations may be criminalized unless Congress has passed a statute specifically making a regulation criminal or incorporating it into 18 United States Code. The law should state that nothing in the CFR may be so incorporated by the Department of Justice. This would eliminate the ability of prosecutors to take federal regulations and criminalize them via the conspiracy or aiding-and-abetting statutes.

2. Congress must eliminate absolute immunity for prosecutors. Remarkably, prosecutors have always enjoyed absolute immunity, even for their intentional misconduct. No one else enjoys such protection—not even police officers and other law enforcement officials who must make split-second life-altering decisions while their adrenaline is pumping. The protection afforded prosecutors has been abused beyond measure.

Both supervisory personnel and bar associations have failed to meet any standard of holding prosecutors accountable for their misconduct. Courts are loath to do so, because often any meaningful action requires reversing a criminal conviction. This must change. We can no longer turn a blind eye to prosecutors' failures to meet their constitutional, ethical, and legal obligations. It is imperative that we provide a means to relief for those who have been damaged by prosecutors' intentional misconduct as a tactic to win at any cost.

It would be a simple matter to create an exception to the Federal Tort Claims Act that allows federal prosecutors to be sued for damages by people who have been wrongly convicted based on evidence that was falsified or manufactured by corrupt prosecutors, or because exculpatory evidence was deliberately withheld. Police officers, who must act in imminent danger, only have qualified immunity. Prosecutors deserve nothing more. They have time for reasoned reflection and great care in making their decisions.

3. No one within the federal government should be protected for any act

of dishonesty or criminal conduct. Federal officials are public servants who work for the taxpayers. Any proven instance of criminal conduct should warrant prompt termination of employment. Government employees should be fired for any violation of the *Brady* rule or any ethical violation involving "lack of candor" to a court, the Justice Department, or any other federal agency. Government officials who break the law must be punished in the same way that citizens outside of government are.

It was appalling to see that a high Justice Department official was recently found to have pornography on his computer, and then he lied about it under oath to the inspector general. Other people have been prosecuted for far less. He simply lost his job.[28] It is time for the Justice Department to prosecute its own just as it would anyone else. No one should get a pass on criminal prosecution because he works for the government. If anything, government employees should be viewed as public servants and held to higher standards—certainly not lower ones.

4. There should be a federal conviction-integrity review unit with a strong measure of independence from the Department of Justice, to review questionable convictions and the conduct of prosecutors. It should be staffed with former prosecutors, defense lawyers, and citizens with some experience of the justice system—perhaps those who have been acquitted or had their wrongful convictions reversed. Retired judges in such review units would add useful experience. They should be allowed to review the convictions of anyone and any case in which there is probable cause to believe that a *Brady* violation occurred—or any other kind of egregious prosecutorial misconduct that caused a wrongful conviction.

5. The authority of the inspector general of the Department of Justice should be increased. As it stands now, he is the weakest inspector general. He should be given additional powers commensurate with the most powerful of the inspectors general. His or her power needs to be equal to the size and seriousness of the problem—and the problems in the Department of Justice, which includes the FBI, have become staggering.

6. Prosecutors should be required to sign an agreement that they will not seek public office for at least three years following their public service. Far too many prosecutors seek high-profile cases to propel their careers and fuel their political ambitions. That is not the proper motivation for a federal prosecutor, whose job is to seek justice—not headlines.

7. All government employees with the exception of the military should be limited to fifteen years of government service. The longer people are entrenched in one position, the less accountability they seem to have, and the more they seem to forget their role as a public servant. This seems especially true recently within the upper ranks of the Department of Justice and the FBI.

CHAPTER EIGHT

WHERE HAVE ALL THE JUDGES GONE?

Federal Courts Have Supervisory Power over Federal Criminal Justice, and It's High Time They Used It

The massive growth in the American prison population has coincided, not surprisingly, with a growing asymmetry in power between the government and the defendant. Ideally, the judiciary should limit the government's power over accused criminals and innocent citizens alike, but unfortunately the bench has increasingly deferred to "the government," embodied in federal agents and prosecutors.

The federal courts have embraced such "avoidance doctrines"[1] as *harmless error* to avoid vacating convictions, and have practiced so-called "judicial modesty" by exercising restraint in their opinions. It is difficult to get a federal court to countenance a claim of prosecutorial misconduct, and nearly impossible to get a court to name in its opinion the prosecutors who have broken the rules. When a court dares to name a federal culprit, the Department of Justice usually requests that the name(s) be removed. Often, and shamefully, courts acquiesce.[2]

As many others have suggested,[3] it is imperative that the federal judiciary reclaim its role as a constitutional check on the executive and legislative branches. To this end, the federal bench should vigorously reassert its "supervisory authority over the administration of criminal justice in the federal courts," as Justice Felix Frankfurter put it in *McNabb v. United States* (1943).[4] It must combat the scourge of prosecutorial and investigative misconduct that has long been tacitly accepted and has fostered the conviction machine.[†]

Justice Frankfurter's famous opinion for the majority in *McNabb* represented the apex of the supervisory powers doctrine in federal criminal jurisprudence, which enables courts to penalize unconstitutional, illegal, or otherwise unacceptable government conduct even in the absence of a defendant with standing to invoke the violated constitutional right. The Supreme Court ruled in a federal murder case that confessions elicited from suspects by unlawful means were inadmissible as evidence against the defendants. The Court promulgated the notion that while specific constitutional rights established a floor beneath which the treatment of a defendant could not fall, there were also other principles enforceable by the federal courts, to be applied more broadly and with fewer technicalities. The courts, Frankfurter wrote, should not be "accomplices in willful disobedience of law" even if "Congress has not explicitly forbidden the use of evidence" procured unlawfully.

The *McNabb* opinion, followed in 1957 by the case of *Mallory v. United States* (also involving the coercive interrogation of a suspect), resulted in a relatively brief period when the so-called "*McNabb/Mallory* rule" encouraged judges to hold agents and prosecutors accountable for tactics deemed unworthy of a civilized criminal justice system. This rule was invoked less frequently, however, after *Miranda v. Arizona* was decided by the Supreme Court in

---

† State courts are powerless to supervise the actions of federal agents and prosecutors, due to the "supremacy clause" of the Constitution, which elevates federal power over state power in the law enforcement arena. State courts may refuse to allow evidence unlawfully acquired (by federal agents) to be admitted in *state* trials, however.

1966, requiring that detained suspects be made aware of their Fifth Amendment privilege against self-incrimination and their right to an attorney. The high court's decision in *Miranda* constitutionalized the issue of coercive, custodial interrogations and moved away from a reliance on supervisory power alone.[5]

Without explicit direction from Congress, the Supreme Court and the federal courts have abandoned or neglected their oversight of our criminal justice system via their supervisory powers. The resulting vacuum has allowed more abuses and lawlessness in the system. The following examples of judicial oversight by the district court, from two very different sorts of criminal prosecutions, illustrate the need for the federal bench to reassert this power.

• • •

"Operation Tradewinds" was an IRS investigation, launched in 1965, that focused in large part on the Castle Bank & Trust in Nassau, Bahamas. The bank was suspected of money laundering and providing a tax haven for wealthy American businessmen, drug traffickers, and the mob (not to mention the CIA, which used it to fund covert operations).[6] After failing to gain any substantial evidence of criminal wrongdoing on the part of the bank's customers, the IRS devised quite the scheme to obtain bank documents from one of the bank's executives, Michael Wolstencroft.

Norman Casper, working as an informant for the government, arranged for Wolstencroft to have dinner with Casper's associate, Sybol Kennedy, when Wolstencroft was visiting Miami for business in 1973. While the two were out to dinner, Casper broke into Kennedy's apartment, where Wolstencroft had left his briefcase, and, without a warrant, seized hundreds of bank documents within it. The IRS photographed the documents before Casper returned them to Kennedy's apartment, leaving Wolstencroft none the wiser. These documents ultimately became the basis for the agency's case against one Jack Payner.

The government indicted Payner for falsifying his federal income tax return, a violation of the infamous federal false-statement statute (Title 18, United States Code, section 1001).[†] Prosecutors claimed that Payner falsely denied that he had a bank account in the Bahamas, despite the fact that several years earlier he had signed a guarantee agreement pledging the funds in a Bahamas account as security for a loan. Since Payner opted for a bench trial, the outcome of the case depended on whether the court would exclude evidence of the existence of the foreign bank account from his trial because it was seized unlawfully, even if it did not violate Payner's constitutional rights.

The issue was eventually decided by the Supreme Court in 1980, in *United States v. Payner*.[7] The question for the Court was whether the bank statements obtained illegally should be excluded from Payner's trial. Under the traditional Supreme Court "exclusionary rule," evidence seized unconstitutionally cannot be used against the *victim* of the unlawful conduct. The victim here was Wolstencroft because it was his briefcase that had been burgled and violated. A victim is the only person who has standing to raise the unconstitutionality of a search-and-seizure. Third parties—in this case, Payner—have no standing to complain, even if the evidence is used against them, since it was not *their* premises or rights that were directly violated. Constitutional violations are, in this sense, deemed personal, rather than systemic.

Payner therefore had no right under the Fourth Amendment to have the evidence suppressed as the fruits of an unconstitutional

---

† 18 U.S.C. § 1001 is the same statute discussed in Chapter 1 in connection with the FBI's use of 302 reports in lieu of recorded interviews. It criminalizes any "material" false statement made to any federal government entity, employee, or agent, even when not under oath, and even when the individual is not given any warning of the penalty for answering falsely (or even *arguably* falsely). The false-statement statute is the quintessential trap for the unwary. Few know that it is a felony to lie to a federal official, even when unsworn, and a "lie" can include failing to remember or recite something the agents think you should—regardless of whether they ask you. Federal agents normally do not record their interrogations, but simply take notes, and the agent's version of what the interviewee said is almost always taken as the more accurate version of the interview—a huge problem and trap.

search. The legal question in his prosecution was whether the evidence had to be excluded for other reasons.

The district court and the Sixth Circuit Court of Appeals, upon discovering the rather extraordinary misconduct and invasion of Wolstencroft's privacy by federal agents, had ordered that the seized evidence be excluded from Payner's trial. The courts relied on their inherent "supervisory power" over the administration of federal criminal justice in making this ruling. Though the search may not have directly violated Payner's rights, the courts found the conduct of the federal agents so offensive to the justice system writ large that they refused to reward that conduct (and thereby encourage it in the future). The Supreme Court, however, disagreed with this application of the court's supervisory powers and reversed the lower courts' exclusionary decision, dooming Payner to a conviction, and undoubtedly encouraging more such illegal conduct by the government.

The basis of the Supreme Court's remarkable willingness to countenance what any neutral observer would deem dishonorable if not outright thuggish conduct on the part of the federal agents was laid out by Justice Lewis Powell, with whom five other members of the high court concurred. The majority paid lip service to the outrage expressed by the lower court judges toward the government's offensive conduct, but it held that the rule excluding evidence wrongly obtained must not be applied "in every case of illegality." The Court was more concerned with punishing criminal conduct of citizens than illegal action by the government.[†] In what has become a frequently used aphorism, it is "the defendant, and not the constable, who stands trial." Or, in a more common formulation: the defendant does not escape simply because "the

---

† Justice Powell warned of "the considerable harm that would flow from indiscriminate application of an exclusionary rule." If evidence, even illegally obtained evidence, were excluded, such enforcement of "ideals of governmental rectitude would impede unacceptably the truth-finding function." Powell believed that the court's mission to discover and punish criminal wrongdoing must be elevated above its duty to check the government in its exercise of that power, even if unlawful. But if those who enforce the laws fail to follow them, there really is no law.

constable blundered." (What is ignored by this aphorism is, of course, the fact that it was not a "blunder" by the constable, but a deliberate, calculated unlawful act that violated the rights of a law-abiding citizen.)

Justice Powell and the majority in *Payner* effectively licensed the ever-increasing heavy-handed treatment of citizens in the federal criminal justice system. The "constable" can do almost anything and is never held accountable. For the most part, he enjoys the absolute immunity of the sovereign. The Court in *Payner* held that the federal courts' inherent "supervisory power over the administration of criminal justice" did not empower the trial judge to exclude the evidence. The records were admitted, the defendant stood convicted, and neither the prosecutor nor the agents were held accountable for their crime. This only further empowers the burgeoning police state and the abuse of individual rights the government is supposed to protect.

The three dissenting justices were understandably furious. They argued that the purpose of the exclusionary rule should be "to deter illegal conduct by Government officials, and to protect the integrity of the federal courts." Drawing fine lines as to who could and who could not invoke the exclusionary rule defeated the purpose of the rule and of the constitutional right, according to the dissenters. "Crime is contagious," they wrote, and if the government is allowed to break the law with impunity, "it invites anarchy." Making their minority position clear, they noted, "The federal judiciary should not be made accomplices to the crimes" of wayward federal agents.

As the law now stands, in the absence of a defendant's technical legal standing to invoke a constitutional right, federal agents can get away with such unlawful searches and seizures against citizens when building a case against a third party. We urge that the *Payner* Court erred in overturning the lower courts' attempts at combatting illegal governmental behavior via the use of its supervisory power. The decision should be overturned either by the current Supreme

Court or through a statutory directive from Congress that prohibits the government from using any evidence it has obtained by breaking the law itself.[†]

• • •

Other federal courts have expressed chagrin or disdain for limitations on their power to insist that federal justice be worthy of the name. Judge John Gleeson, sitting in the Eastern District of New York in Brooklyn, engaged in mildly rebellious judicial conduct by insisting on maintaining supervision when he presided over a 2012 bank fraud prosecution of HSBC Holdings. The international financial services corporation was charged with violating its obligations to report to the federal government certain suspicious monetary transactions made by customers. Pleading guilty to that felonious conduct could have crippled many if not all the bank's operations. The Department of Justice allowed HSBC instead to enter into a prenegotiated deferred prosecution agreement (DPA) to settle the matter without a conviction. The DPA was filed along with its traditional sister agreement, a corporate compliance monitor (CCM) agreement.[‡]

These two agreements, taken together, follow a certain paradigm developed by the Department of Justice and routinely approved by the federal courts. The arrangement here was typical: the government agreed to forgo obtaining a formal grand jury indictment of the bank, and the bank agreed to correct its illegal behavior under

---

† Some will argue that the system should rely on disciplining or prosecuting agents when they misbehave, rather than invoking the exclusionary rule that "rewards" criminals because the constable blundered or even intentionally misbehaved. However, disciplining or prosecuting errant prosecutors or agents virtually never happens, and if it does at all, it is a hit-or-miss remedy. Procedures for disciplining agents and attorneys are belabored with so many rules and regulations that they do no good. Moreover, the proceedings are usually secret and confidential. Neither the public nor the courts know if or when an errant agent has been sanctioned—even if there were a blatant violation of law. Often such sanctions are laughably lenient. One example is the aftermath of the gross prosecutorial misconduct employed to obtain the guilty verdict against Senator Ted Stevens, discussed in Chapter 3.

‡ The government began using this paired tactic frequently after its indictment of Arthur Andersen LLP completely and immediately destroyed the venerable accounting firm. See Powell, *Licensed to Lie.*

the guidance of an independent monitor. Since that meant a delay extending the case beyond the statute of limitations, HSBC agreed to suspend its legal right to a timely indictment. The bank further agreed to take certain steps to assure the government that its unlawful conduct would not recur. If the bank adhered to the agreement for the full period of the diversion, the charges would be dropped at the end of the process. Thus, the bank would never be indicted, and it would not suffer the often debilitating and quite possibly fatal regulatory and reputational consequences that accompany an indictment.†

The mere threat of criminal charges against a highly regulated financial institution puts the company at the mercy of the Department of Justice, which wields the power to destroy it. Recent cases suggest that these institutions will do virtually anything asked of them by federal prosecutors, including betray their employees and even provide evidence and testimony of questionable veracity.[8]

When Judge Gleeson announced that he would approve the DPA only on the condition that he retain jurisdiction to monitor its execution over its five-year term, it evidently came as a surprise both to the DOJ and to HSBC. Yet it is easy to see why he insisted on maintaining supervision. Gleeson specifically invoked the court's "authority to approve or reject the DPA pursuant to its supervisory power," and cited *McNabb*, emphasizing the Supreme Court's insistence that it "fashion civilized standards of procedure and evidence applicable to federal criminal proceedings."[9]

The goal of such judicial monitoring, wrote Judge Gleeson, was "to preserve the integrity of the judicial process." Ironically, both

---

† The case of Arthur Andersen is a dramatic example of the destructive impact an indictment can have on a banking institution that depends upon a clean bill of health to operate in a highly regulated state, federal, and international financial environment. Arthur Andersen LLP, one of the five largest accounting and auditing firms in the United States, was indicted in 2002 for obstruction of justice in connection with its audit of Enron. The government knew the indictment was a death penalty for Andersen, so the indictment was sealed for a week while the government worked behind the scenes to avoid upheaval in the financial markets. When the indictment was announced, hundreds of civil litigants piled on. By the time the Supreme Court unanimously reversed the conviction, the firm was long gone. The story is told in Silverglate, *Three Felonies a Day*, chap. 5, and in Powell, *Licensed to Lie*, chap. 3.

the government and the bank disagreed, asserting that Gleeson's role should be limited to deciding whether to dismiss the charges against HSBC once the DPA expired. Gleeson rejected such a petty ministerial role for the judiciary, and such an absolute and unsupervised role for the prosecutors. He cited the "public relations benefits" to both the bank and the Department of Justice in maintaining a non-prosecution agreement, and he affirmed that "a pending federal criminal case is not window dressing. Nor is the Court, to borrow a famous phrase, a potted plant." Since the court was being asked to put its imprimatur on the settlement of the case, it would insist on playing an active role in monitoring the agreement not only to protect the parties, but, importantly, "to protect the integrity of the Court."

In a footnote, Judge Gleeson recounted how, in prior DPAs, corporations were coerced into performing actions that would violate certain rights of their employees and others. It is likely that Gleeson saw fit to justify his conduct in a written opinion because he was aware that his assertion of judicial authority was controversial. The Department of Justice, after all, was conferring major benefits on a corporate cooperator in exchange for the corporation's doing the DOJ's bidding. Was it proper, he wondered, for the court's supervision to be eliminated from the balance?

Judge Gleeson's cautiousness proved wise. Not long after this decision, when another judge sought to invoke supervisory authority over a case, he was appealed and reversed in the circuit court. That judge was Richard J. Leon of the United States District Court for the District of Columbia, in the case of *United States v. Fokker Services B.V.*[10] Fokker was "charged with a five-year conspiracy to violate and evade United States export laws for the benefit, largely, of Iran and its military during the post-9/11 world when we were engaged in a two-front War against terror in the Middle East."[11] Judge Leon denied outright the government's motion to exclude the case from the Speedy Trial Act's time limit. He was acting, he said, out of consideration for "the integrity of the judicial process."

Like Gleeson, Judge Leon insisted that the "court must consider the public as well as the defendant" if it is to be asked to "lend its judicial imprimatur to [a] DPA."

Unfortunately, even this modest exercise of judicial oversight to maintain the integrity of the justice system was overturned by the Court of Appeals for the District of Columbia Circuit. The court ruled that charging decisions are the exclusive purview of the executive branch and that Judge Leon's denial of the DPA, on the grounds that its terms weren't severe enough on the defendant and involved inadequate monitoring by the court, was a breach of that governmental authority. The court of appeals entirely ignored Leon's language invoking supervisory authority, and instead it focused narrowly on the Speedy Trial Act statute as it was written, noting: "Nothing in the statute's terms or structure suggests any intention to subvert those constitutionally rooted principles so as to enable the Judiciary to second-guess the Executive's exercise of discretion over the initiation and dismissal of criminal charges."[12]

In his decision, Judge Leon recognized the government's role in charging defendants and admitted that the bench should exercise its supervisory authority "sparingly." Nonetheless, he refused to accept the terms of the DPA due to the egregious misconduct of Fokker. Having made $21 million selling aviation parts and technology to Iran, Sudan, and Burma during times of U.S. sanctions against those governments, Fokker was being offered a settlement that would see not a single employee indicted and would allow the company to implement compliance measures for eighteen months without any governmental oversight. Fokker would not be fined "a penny more than the $21 million in revenue it collected from its illegal transactions."[13] Despite Judge Leon's clearly expressed concerns about the effect of this settlement on the integrity of American criminal justice, he was overturned by the court of appeals and denied his ability to exercise his supervisory authority over the deal.

The supervisory power of the federal courts is an important power that warrants a revival to protect the integrity of the system.

The most recent and egregious example of the government's abuse of its power in the system is the apparent fraud on the courts that operate pursuant to the Foreign Intelligence Surveillance Act.[14] These courts are super-secret. Any defendant who is brought before them is not allowed to have counsel or tell anyone about his case. It is as un-American—as much like a "star chamber"—as anyone might imagine. The use and abuse of these courts has grown astronomically since 9/11, culminating in their recent issuance by four different judges of the most intrusive of all warrants against Carter W. Page, American citizen and former naval officer, on the basis of a completely bogus application most of which was bought and paid for by the campaign of Hillary Clinton and the Democratic National Committee through the law firm of Perkins Coie and the private company Fusion GPS. The scheme also required the full cooperation of the upper echelon of the FBI and the Department of Justice. At the time of this writing, we still await the reportedly massive report of the inspector general on the FISA abuses, and the Department of Justice has opened a criminal investigation into the matter.

The problem is much more widespread than this, however. Two FISA judges have issued significant decisions which, although heavily redacted, reveal egregious Fourth Amendment violations by the FBI, the NSA, the Department of Justice, and others who have used our government data collection systems for political purposes. All the while, the FISA courts have done little to nothing under their statutory powers and even less under their supervisory powers to hold the abusers in contempt, to reject warrant applications, or anything else to stem the tide of abuses.[15]

◆ ◆ ◆

The federal judiciary's extreme reluctance to rely on supervisory power generally reflects a hesitancy to deal directly and forcefully with federal investigative misconduct and prosecutorial overreach. What is often overlooked is that the court's truth-seeking function is compromised when agents act illegally to build a case, even in the absence of a direct constitutional violation. Moreover, the dignity of federal court proceedings is undoubtedly diminished when the rule of force, or raw power, replaces the rule of law, and when agents are permitted to flout the law without accountability or any repercussion.

The Founders created the federal judiciary as a separate and equal branch of government for a reason. Surely the time has come when the federal courts' power to supervise the administration of criminal justice should be robust and beyond doubt—not hampered by undue "judicial modesty." One scholar reviewed the history of the Supreme Court's on-again, off-again resort to the supervisory power, and, while concluding that such supervisory power exists, recognized that Congress may have to legislate a specific grant of such power to the Supreme Court.[16]

Alternatively, in the absence of the Supreme Court's effectively exercised general supervision over federal justice, it is up to Congress to enact legislation conferring on the federal district courts the clear power, and indeed the affirmative obligation, to prohibit some of the more egregious examples of prosecutorial overreach, to oversee the details of deferred prosecution agreements and other such exercises of law enforcement power, and generally to enforce constitutional rights and other elements of fairness that exist in this country to *protect the individual from* the government. There is no question that the bench should play a more active role in reviewing and even dictating the line between proper and improper investigative and prosecutorial tactics, to cabin the power of law enforcement officers and prosecutors, prevent and punish investigative and prosecutorial misconduct, and ensure that our justice system is, in fact, honest and just.

CHAPTER NINE

ONCE IS NOT ENOUGH

Restore habeas corpus *and* coram nobis,
*Repeal the Antiterrorism and
Effective Death Penalty Act of 1996*

W hen Congress passed the Antiterrorism and Effective Death Penalty Act (AEDPA) in 1996, it added a provision that eliminated the ability of defendants to seek post-conviction relief pursuant to one of the oldest means in law—the writ of *habeas corpus*. The provision is causing innumerable injustices and making it far too difficult to correct clear wrongs in the justice system.

The case of Jeffrey MacDonald illustrates the problem. In 1989, this co-author, Harvey Silverglate, received a phone call from Dr. MacDonald, a federal prisoner who, perhaps in order to get my attention, identified himself as a fellow Princeton alumnus. We did not know each other while on campus; MacDonald graduated a year ahead of me, and we traveled in decidedly different circles. But by the time MacDonald called, I knew who he was. He had been convicted of the 1970 "Green Beret murders" of his pregnant wife and two young daughters, in a highly publicized trial in 1979. A bestselling book on the case,[1] soon turned into a movie,[2] largely convinced the public that MacDonald was guilty. He insisted on his innocence, and claimed that his prosecution was unconstitutional.

And he wanted me and my longtime friend and mentor, Professor Alan Dershowitz of Harvard Law School, to help him prove it.

The case was in the post-conviction stage. MacDonald had exhausted his direct appeals, and he had already filed, in 1984, one unsuccessful post-conviction petition asking the courts to issue a writ of *habeas corpus*. Even in 1989, I knew that federal *habeas* law was a thicket of complex rules and regulations, and that success was a long shot. I took the case regardless. Little did I know that in less than a decade, the light at the end of a wrongfully convicted prisoner's tunnel—a writ of *habeas corpus*—would shrink to a pinprick. Congress and the federal courts have gutted one of American prisoners' oldest rights, and Jeffrey MacDonald and countless others have suffered because of it.

◆   ◆   ◆

The doctrine of *habeas corpus* exists as a safety valve for the wrongfully convicted. In theory, if a prisoner believes he is being detained unlawfully, he can petition the court to issue a writ of *habeas corpus*, which commands the jailer to bring the prisoner to court (*habeas corpus* means literally, "that you have the body") so that a judge can decide if the imprisonment is justified. This doctrine is crucial in preventing governments from unduly infringing on the liberties of its citizens. In a society with robust *habeas* protections, a sovereign cannot toss his enemies and critics into the proverbial cold, dank cell and figuratively throw away the key.

Habeas corpus comes to us from our common law heritage, meaning it existed in England long before the formation of the United States. Our Founding Fathers intended to preserve *habeas corpus* in their new republic. The "suspension clause" in Article I of the Constitution reads, "The Privilege of the Writ of Habeas Corpus shall not be suspended, unless when in Cases of Rebellion or Invasion the public Safety may require it."[3] To give this constitutional promise teeth, the first United States Congress passed the Judiciary Act in 1789. In addition to prescribing the features of a federal judiciary, Section 14 of the act, sometimes called the "All Writs Act," included broad language that vested the judiciary with tremendous power. It declared that federal courts could issue writs of *habeas corpus*, "and all other writs not specially provided for by statute, which may be necessary for the exercise of their respective jurisdictions, and agreeable to the principles and usages of law."[4] Congress's intention was clear: courts were to serve as a bulwark against government by using their expansive power to uphold "the principles and usages of law."[5]

Habeas corpus doctrine has been a mainstay of English and later American liberty for centuries. Indeed, it is often referred to as the "Great Writ." In recent decades, however, *habeas corpus* and other post-conviction remedies have been so severely restricted in their use that, more and more frequently, when the steel door of the prison cell closes, it closes for good (or until the prisoner's release date).

Severe narrowing of this crucial doctrine began in earnest in 1991 with the Supreme Court decision *McCleskey v. Zant,* which held that prisoners have the right to file only one *habeas* petition; successive petitions would henceforth be almost impossible.[6] This opinion was codified in the onerous Antiterrorism and Effective Death Penalty Act (AEDPA) of 1996, which also added complex procedural requirements and placed a one-year time limit on filing motions under 28 U.S.C. § 2255, the federal statute that currently serves as the avenue for federal prisoners to seek *habeas* relief.[7] AEDPA also imposed corresponding restrictions on motions pursuant to 28 U.S.C. § 2244, the *habeas corpus* statute for state prisoners. These semi-recent developments are taking a huge and likely irrevocable toll on liberty, fairness, and due process of law. They make it extraordinarily difficult for prisoners to attack the all-too-common wrongful conviction.

◆　◆　◆

By the time I (Silverglate) came into Jeffrey MacDonald's case in 1989, he had been living a nightmare for almost twenty years. In

February 1970, military police entered the young Green Beret surgeon's home in Fort Bragg, North Carolina, to find MacDonald's wife, Collette, and their two daughters savagely slain. MacDonald was himself badly injured. He later told investigators that the perpetrators were four intruders, dressed like hippies and possibly on psychedelic acid, and that he struggled with some of them, lost consciousness, and woke up to the gruesome murder scene.

MacDonald's story seemed strange to investigators—almost too reminiscent of the Charles Manson murders that had occurred in the late 1960s—but it was partially corroborated by members of law enforcement. One first responder reported seeing a woman matching MacDonald's description of the female intruder by the side of the road when he was driving to the crime scene; another detective thought perhaps the woman was Helena Stoeckley, a local drug informant.[†]

Nevertheless, MacDonald became the prime suspect. He was cleared at an Article 32 hearing—a military procedure to determine which, if any, charges should be brought. He left the army to pursue a career as a surgeon in California. But almost a decade later, civilian federal prosecutors indicted him for the murders of his wife and daughters and secured a conviction in 1979. MacDonald was sentenced to consecutive life sentences and is still incarcerated today.[8]

One of our first acts as MacDonald's new lawyers (the core team consisted of attorneys Andrew Good and Phillip Cormier, law professor Alan Dershowitz, and myself) was to review the voluminous case file. In advance of MacDonald's first unsuccessful *habeas* petition, filed some five years earlier, the government had turned over thousands of documents requested under the Freedom of Information Act (FOIA).

One of the documents discovered by the FOIA experts was particularly noteworthy. It was a legal research memorandum written by a law student intern answering several legal questions from one

† Helena Stoeckley would later confess multiple times to being one of the intruders in MacDonald's home on the night of the murders. She died in 1983.

of the trial prosecutors: Which categories of evidence had to be turned over, and what could be withheld? The formulation of the questions that the prosecutor asked the student to research gave me the sense that the prosecutor had come across evidence that he did not want to turn over and was looking for a legal basis for defending that decision, particularly if his judgment was later questioned. Among the documents *withheld* were forensic laboratory notes that could lead to a conclusion that the murders were committed not by MacDonald, but by strangers who had entered the apartment.

The MacDonald post-conviction *habeas corpus* team was buoyed by these discoveries, which, when added to the considerable collection of evidence uncovered since the jury verdict, appeared to present an overwhelming argument for the judge's vacating the conviction and sentence that he had imposed ten years earlier. By 1990, we thought that we could draft a powerful petition for a writ of *habeas corpus* that would, once and for all, get MacDonald a new trial. At such a retrial, we were confident, any jury would acquit. The evidence seemed to be multiplying by the day—implicating the hippie band and exculpating MacDonald.

We filed our *habeas* petition in October 1990, the government filed its opposition, and we prepared our reply brief. In the face of the newly discovered evidence, we figured that even the hostile North Carolina federal judge would not be able to find a way to deny us an evidentiary hearing at which we could present our cache of evidence and examine government agents, lawyers, and experts to inquire as to why this evidence was not presented at the time of MacDonald's trial.

But in April 1991, something devastatingly transformative occurred in the arena of *habeas corpus* law.

Just as we were preparing to file our reply brief, I got a phone call from a colleague informing me that the Supreme Court had released its decision in the case of *McCleskey v. Zant*. The opinion, which remains the controlling law today, held that defendants have the right to file only one *habeas* petition. Going forward, any additional petitions would face numerous procedural obstacles. For one, the prisoner would have to explain why he did not file the new evidence in his first *habeas* petition and demonstrate "actual innocence" simply to get an evidentiary hearing. In short, it was no longer sufficient to show that a defendant had an unconstitutionally unfair trial; he would also have to show, *before* being given a forum to subpoena documents and witnesses, that he was innocent, or at least that "a fundamental miscarriage of justice would result from a failure to entertain the claim."[9]

Several months after the Supreme Court's decision undermining a prisoner's access to *habeas corpus* was released, Judge Franklin Dupree (the same judge who oversaw MacDonald's original trial) denied our motion for a new trial, citing *McCleskey*. When we appealed Judge Dupree's decision, the Fourth Circuit Court of Appeals said that MacDonald should have discovered and presented his new evidence in his first *habeas* petition, back in 1984—never mind that this would have been impossible. In 1992, the U.S. Supreme Court declined to review the case. We knew we had a good case, but changes in *habeas* law meant that our petitions were denied on procedural grounds—not on the merits.

But we kept trying, and MacDonald's appeals bounced around the courts for years. Unhelpfully, in 1996, in a frenzied response to both the first World Trade Center terrorist attack in New York City and the Oklahoma City bombing, Congress enacted the Antiterrorism and Effective Death Penalty Act, which codified in legislation the limitations on *habeas corpus* set forth by the Supreme Court in *McCleskey*, and even added several more. Each time the *habeas* petition was denied, we sought review in the Fourth Circuit, and each time, the Fourth Circuit affirmed the district court—until, that is, the appellate court suddenly recognized the overwhelming amount of evidence produced by MacDonald (and kept hidden by the prosecutors and other government agents).

Consequently, on April 19, 2011, in a sharp break from the spirit of *McCleskey* and AEDPA, the Fourth Circuit finally ordered the district court to hold a hearing at which witnesses could be called, sworn, and forced to testify.[10] Technically, the appellate court could again have refused to order that a hearing be convened, but apparently the judges were beginning to feel uncomfortable with the status quo that the *McCleskey* opinion and the AEDPA statute appeared to mandate. The Fourth Circuit ordered the lower court to hold a hearing where the *totality* of accumulated evidence could be evaluated. Finally, a glimmer of hope—the hearing was held in September 2012.

Unfortunately, on July 24, 2014, Judge James C. Fox (who took over the MacDonald case after Judge Dupree's death in 1995) denied MacDonald's *habeas* petition.[11] His most recent denial of a new trial took place in December 2018. It is unlikely that MacDonald, who was born in 1943, will see justice any time soon. He remains in prison; just one casualty of Congress's and the federal courts' complete trampling of the once Great Writ that existed for the very purpose of avoiding egregious miscarriages of justice—especially when new information belatedly comes to light.

• • •

Congress needs to lighten its restrictions on *habeas corpus*, at a minimum, to allow for a second writ upon discovery of new evidence or upon discovery of any government misconduct such as withholding evidence, whether intentional or unintentional. In addition, Congress or the Supreme Court needs to resurrect the writ of error *coram nobis*. While *habeas corpus* is the most well-known post-conviction remedy, even at its most robust it could not rectify every miscarriage of justice.

The Great Writ was always intended to protect individuals against wrongful detention, and therefore it applies only to those physically in custody.† But the consequences of a wrongful conviction are not limited to jail time. A criminal record follows an

---

† The statute under which federal prisoners attack their convictions, 28 U.S.C. § 2255, applies specifically to "a prisoner in custody."

individual the rest of his life. Our English forebears recognized that there must be an avenue for overturning a wrongful conviction even if the person petitioning the court for relief is no longer being detained. Out of this necessity, the courts developed the doctrine of *coram nobis*.

Coram nobis functions much the same as *habeas corpus*: it allows a petitioner to present new facts or evidence in hopes of reversing an otherwise final judgment. Like *habeas corpus*, the *coram nobis* doctrine was incorporated into American jurisprudence by way of the Judiciary Act of 1789, under the Section 14 All Writs Act. *Coram nobis* existed in theory, but not really in practice, until 1954, when the Supreme Court in *United States v. Morgan* affirmed the Second Circuit Court of Appeals ruling that the writ was available to those convicted in federal courts. The high court recognized, however, that *coram nobis* relief should be granted only in extraordinary circumstances; it was a writ of last resort, designed to rectify errors "of the most fundamental character."[12]

By opening another post-conviction avenue besides *habeas corpus* for individuals to attack wrongful convictions, the Supreme Court essentially admitted that our judicial system makes mistakes, and that corrective measures need to be available. But like *habeas* doctrine, *coram nobis* has been kneecapped in the years since *Morgan*, and sadly, it has been the federal courts, not the legislative branch, that have narrowed access to this crucial writ.

For a dramatic example of the importance of *coram nobis* doctrine, one need look no further than the case of Fred Korematsu. During World War II, several cases involving the constitutionality of Japanese internment and relocation made their way to the Supreme Court. The most famous of these cases was perhaps *Korematsu v. United States* (1944), in which Korematsu, a young man of Japanese ancestry, attacked the constitutionality of a military order that required him to leave his home. This military order, Civilian Exclusion Order No. 34, was authorized under President Franklin D. Roosevelt's Executive Order 9066, which gave the military sweeping power to relocate and indefinitely detain large numbers of Japanese Americans. Korematsu refused to leave his home and report to the required "relocation center." He was convicted of violating the order, and the Supreme Court upheld his conviction, as it had done in a similar case the year before. Justice Frank Murphy, in an anguished, unvarnished, powerful dissent, accused the federal government and the high court's majority of exceeding "the very brink of constitutional power" and of falling "into the ugly abyss of racism."[13]

Several decades later, it seemed that conscience finally caught up to the U.S. government. In 1980, Congress established the Commission on Wartime Relocation and Internment of Civilians to reexamine policies of the Roosevelt administration that led to mass detention of Japanese Americans. In 1983, the commission released a report titled "Personal Justice Denied," which contained shocking revelations about how these racially motivated policies had survived constitutional challenges.

In the *Korematsu* case and its predecessor, *United States v. Hirabayashi* (1943), the Supreme Court had upheld civilian exclusion orders largely on the basis of a 1943 report by Lieutenant General J. L. DeWitt, who at the time was in charge of the security of the entire West Coast of the United States.[14] He wrote in his report to the secretary of war, Henry Stimson, that detention of Japanese Americans was necessary to prevent another attack or an invasion by imperial Japan. Specifically, General DeWitt cited instances of signaling from the shore to enemy submarines as evidence of collaboration. But as the "Personal Justice Denied" report would reveal, any allegations of signaling had been investigated and *debunked* by the FBI by the time the Department of Justice presented the DeWitt Report to the Supreme Court in the *Hirabayashi* and *Korematsu* cases.[15]

An independent investigation by Peter Irons, a historian and lawyer, also in the early 1980s, revealed even more of the sordid story. Back in 1943, a young DOJ lawyer named Edward Ennis heard about his colleagues' strategy to win the *Hirabayashi* case and decided to dig into the details of the DeWitt Report. He discovered that investigations by the FBI and the Federal Communications Commission had corroborated *none* of the examples of shore-to-submarine espionage cited in the DeWitt Report. Moreover, he came upon the Office of Naval Intelligence's Ringle Report, which directly contradicted General DeWitt's sweeping claims about Japanese Americans' "racial affinity" for imperial Japan. The Ringle Report estimated that only a tiny percentage of Japanese Americans might be spies, and that "the entire 'Japanese Problem' has been magnified out of its true proportion."[16]

Ennis's findings were ignored and effectively suppressed, and the Supreme Court decided the *Hirabayashi* and *Korematsu* cases largely based on the inaccurate and incomplete information in the DeWitt Report. But Ennis had detailed his findings in an internal memo that never saw the light of day, and when Irons found it almost forty years later, he blew the whole case wide open.[17]

Irons helped Korematsu, by then in his sixties, assemble a legal team to attack his World War II–era conviction. It was too late for Korematsu to file a petition for a writ of *habeas corpus*, as he was no longer under any form of restraint of his personal liberty. His only avenue, then, was to file a petition for a writ of *coram nobis* in federal court. Shamefully, government lawyers opposed this strategy, moving instead to dismiss all the past proceedings and to vacate the result, as if the criminal proceedings had never taken place.[†]

The presiding judge, Marilyn Hall Patel, rejected the government's argument and instead accepted Korematsu's contention that a writ of *coram nobis* was the most appropriate way to right the wrongs inflicted upon him. Judge Patel found that Korematsu's conviction rested on significant government errors that were outlined in the "Personal Justice Denied" report—and crucially not contested by the government. In particular, she determined that DOJ lawyers'

---

† The DOJ even offered Korematsu a pardon in exchange for his dropping the proceedings against the government. He refused.

use of the DeWitt Report in their Supreme Court briefs (and their suppression of all information that contradicted it) resulted in the Court "[having] before it a selective record." This was enough, she ruled, to justify Korematsu's claim for *coram nobis* relief.

To get that relief, however, Korematsu had to prove that he suffered from "collateral consequences…from the fact of a criminal conviction." Judge Patel accepted Korematsu's claim that he was damaged, and would continue to be damaged, from the fact of his conviction, even though he was no longer in prison or on probation. She ruled that he had suffered "a complete miscarriage of justice" and that the "exceptional circumstances" justified the invocation of this extraordinary remedy.

In her opinion clearing his name, Judge Patel wrote that the Korematsu case "stands as a constant caution that in times of war or declared military necessity our institutions must be vigilant in protecting constitutional guarantees."[18]

It wasn't until six years after Korematsu's death that Japanese Americans would receive a formal apology from the Department of Justice. On May 20, 2011, the acting solicitor general of the United States, Neal Katyal, issued a formal "Confession of Error" for his predecessor's conduct during the *Korematsu* and *Hirabayashi* cases. "There are several terrific accounts of the roles that Solicitors General have played throughout history in advancing civil rights," he stated. "But it is also important to remember the mistakes."[19]

Fred Korematsu was lucky. Not only did he have evidence of a massive fraud perpetrated on the Supreme Court by the Department of Justice, but he also landed in front of the right judge. Patel relied on the decision in *United States v. Morgan* (1954) to determine that Korematsu was entitled to *coram nobis* relief, paving the way for the Ninth Circuit Court of Appeals to grant the same relief to Gordon Hirabayashi in 1987. The Ninth Circuit's position on *coram nobis* was solidified in fairly simple terms: a petitioner is entitled to relief if a new fact arises that would have changed the outcome of the case.[20]

Other circuits have interpreted *Morgan* differently, and consequently it is much harder to obtain *coram nobis* relief outside of the Ninth Circuit.[21] A few years after Judge Patel's ruling in Korematsu's case, Judge Frank Easterbrook of the Seventh Circuit Court of Appeals issued an opinion in *United States v. Keane* (1988) that narrowed *coram nobis* doctrine significantly. Under Judge Easterbrook's interpretation of *Morgan*, it was not enough to show new facts or governmental error; a petitioner for a writ of *coram nobis* had to demonstrate that he suffered from "lingering civil disabilities" from his conviction to obtain relief. Reputational or financial injury was not enough. Easterbrook concluded that Keane had failed a strict "civil disabilities test" (created by the judge himself), and he denied the petition.

Unfortunately, the majority of circuit courts have adopted the Seventh Circuit's narrow *coram nobis* doctrine rather than the Ninth Circuit's more expansive one.[22] If Fred Korematsu had brought his case a few years later in a different jurisdiction, perhaps he would have failed the "civil disabilities test" and been denied the legal vindication he deserved. The availability of a writ of *coram nobis* serves as a necessary check on governmental power over citizens; it must be available to those subjected to wrongful convictions, regardless of where in the country they reside. The Supreme Court has not addressed the issue. It remains the task of practitioners to litigate it vigorously.

• • •

Just about every twist and turn of Lord Conrad Black's fraud prosecution reveals another deficiency of the federal criminal justice system—including his experience seeking post-conviction relief. Black's foray into *habeas corpus* and *coram nobis* law highlights a grave issue detrimental to the fair and effective application of post-conviction judicial review. It is easily fixable, though. Post-conviction appeals should not be heard by the same judge who oversaw the original case. It is far too difficult for a federal judge to overturn himself. It happens occasionally, but not with sufficient regularity to be the standard.

Jeffrey MacDonald encountered this reality many times throughout his ordeal; certainly, dealing with individuals who long ago decided on his guilt has stymied his appeals process.† For Conrad Black, repeatedly appearing before Judge Amy St. Eve in the Northern District of Illinois denied his access to justice.

A British businessman, Conrad Black had long led a glamorous life. He ran Hollinger International, a Chicago-based newspaper publishing empire, and he authored several biographies and other works of historical nonfiction. He also was a member of the British House of Lords (granted the title, "The Lord Black of Crossharbour") and an Officer of the Order of Canada. His legal problems began in 2003, when a faction of Hollinger shareholders hired the former chairman of the United States Securities and Exchange Commission (SEC), Richard Breeden, to investigate certain deals that Black and several associates were making on behalf of the company.[23]

Since the late 1990s, Black had—with the board's approval—begun to sell many of the smaller newspapers that Hollinger owned around the world. In many of these sales, Black and his cohorts received a bit more of the sale proceeds than their percentages of stock would otherwise entitle them to get. Black asserted that the bonus was compensation for his agreement with the buyer that he would not compete with the enterprise he was selling.[24] Certain Hollinger shareholders believed that these bonuses were improper, and on Breeden's recommendation, the board of directors forced Black out of his role as Hollinger CEO in 2003.[25]

Two years later, Black was indicted by federal prosecutors in Chicago on charges stemming from the Breeden investigation. In an eleven-count indictment, prosecutors specifically alleged that

---

† Fred Korematsu obviously dealt with a different judge—and a radically different political climate—when he petitioned the court for a writ of *coram nobis*, but that was simply because of the amount of time that had passed since his original conviction.

in 2000, Black and three associates stole millions from Hollinger during the course of a multibillion-dollar sale of assets to a Canadian media company.[26] In 2007, a Chicago jury acquitted Black of most of the government's charges, but convicted him on three counts of mail fraud and one count of obstruction of justice. Judge St. Eve sentenced Black to seventy-eight months in federal prison.[27]

As in many federal white-collar prosecutions, the details of Black's case were extremely complicated. Often, the prosecutors who allege that conduct is criminal don't understand the business transactions at all. In many cases, they have indicted businessmen for conduct that in fact is not criminal (as documented in *Licensed to Lie*). It's difficult enough for the average juror to understand the complexities of corporate mergers and acquisitions; further determining whether the charged conduct violates murky federal statutes is a Herculean task. It is because of this enormous burden on jurors that a judge's instructions, delivered before the jury retreats into deliberations, are so important. It is the judge's duty to instruct the jurors on the law; to tell them *exactly* what the government must prove to find the defendant guilty.

During Black's appeal process in June 2010, the U.S. Supreme Court ruled that Judge St. Eve had incorrectly instructed the jury on "honest services fraud," which was the basis for two of the mail fraud counts on which Black was convicted. According to the Court, the judge's and the prosecutor's broad interpretation of "honest services fraud" was unconstitutionally vague.[28] As a result of this decision, a three-judge panel of the Seventh Circuit Court of Appeals, to which the case was returned after the Supreme Court's decision, overturned part of Black's conviction later that year.

In June 2011, Black again appeared before St. Eve—the same judge who had devised the unconstitutional jury instruction—for resentencing. Despite the evisceration of the meat of Black's conviction on appeal, Judge St. Eve lowered his sentence by a mere three years, to forty-two months. Black got credit for the two years he had already served, but after resentencing he had to return to federal prison for the remainder of his sentence.[29] This time, he was unsuccessful in trying to convince the Supreme Court to review again what the lower courts had done to him.

When Black finally emerged from prison in May 2012, he was still subject to certain conditions of release. What was more damaging, though, was the fact that he was now branded a convicted felon. He had been partially vindicated in the courts, but he wanted to clear his name completely, as he maintained that he had done nothing illegal. Having no further direct appeals available, Black turned to the possibility of *habeas corpus* or *coram nobis* relief. But it would be an uphill climb, as he would have to present his arguments to Judge St. Eve, who had preconceived notions about his guilt, had sentenced him twice, and was perhaps smarting from the Supreme Court's condemnation of her jury instructions in his trial.

Although Black was no longer in federal prison, he was still under "supervised release." It was unclear to his lawyers whether "supervised release" meant he was still technically "in custody" and thus eligible for *habeas corpus* relief. To cover his bases, Black filed a motion for a writ of *habeas corpus*, and also a companion writ of *coram nobis* in case Judge St. Eve found that he was not sufficiently "in custody." Black selected an issue that arose at the very start of the case and that he believed had a giant impact at every subsequent step.

When the government's investigation opened and it was obvious that the feds were after him, Black early on selected as his counsel the renowned Washington, D.C. law firm Williams & Connolly. The lawyer that Black wanted to hire, Brendan V. Sullivan, Jr., was quite pricy, and so Black arranged to sell his New York apartment and use the proceeds of the sale to retain the firm. But just as the apartment sale was closing, the feds seized the proceeds, claiming that the money was "tainted" by Black's alleged fraud and hence subject to forfeiture.[30] Black was thus prevented from retaining the counsel of his choice, a right guaranteed under the Sixth Amendment of the U.S. Constitution.[31] The "deprivation of counsel of choice" claim was buttressed by the related claim that the seizure of the apartment sale proceeds constituted an unreasonable seizure of his property, in violation of the Fourth Amendment, and that all of this together deprived him of due process of law guaranteed by the Fifth Amendment.[32]

In her written opinion, Judge St. Eve determined that Black was sufficiently "in custody" to petition for *habeas* relief, but nevertheless his foray into the once Great Writ proved futile. As to the "deprivation of counsel of choice" claim, St. Eve suddenly had nothing but nice things to say about Black's trial lawyers. She noted that "Petitioner's trial and appellate counsel were some of the most talented and well-respected attorneys in their field."[33] Furthermore, she determined that Black had "procedurally defaulted" on his claims, and so she refused to consider them on their merits.

And just to administer a coup de grâce to Black's effort to reveal and contest the FBI's misconduct and clear his name, Judge St. Eve exercised her "discretion" to deny Black an evidentiary hearing at which he could call witnesses—including the government agents and prosecutors who had orchestrated the suspiciously timed seizure of his apartment sale proceeds—as "the record in this matter conclusively establishes that Petitioner is not entitled to relief under 28 U.S.C. § 2255 because he procedurally defaulted all his claims." More outrageously, St. Eve declared that her decision was not appealable; under the maze that *habeas corpus* law had become, Black couldn't ask the Seventh Circuit to review the judge's decision without her permission.

Does anyone really think Judge St. Eve, at that point, was an impartial arbiter? Just like the prosecutors, she had an interest in upholding Black's conviction; she was the original trial judge, after all. Either consciously or unconsciously, this interest colored her view of Black and his claims. Justice Felix Frankfurter once wrote, "Justice must satisfy the appearance of justice." This did not.

When asked why he didn't take the matter further, Black said that he'd just had enough of what he deemed a "corrupt" legal system. Luckily for Black, in May 2019, more than a decade after his conviction, President Donald Trump granted him a full pardon. The two men have long been close. Most wrongfully convicted defendants, who do not have a friend in the Oval Office, are less lucky.

• • •

Rules of procedure have been the death knell for the writs of *habeas corpus* and *coram nobis*, but we can restore the substance of the great writs with simple fixes.

For one thing, the provisions of the Antiterrorism and Effective Death Penalty Act affecting the writ of *habeas* would have to be substantially revised, if not repealed altogether. One aspect of the law that strikes us as particularly pernicious is the requirement that a petitioner show "actual innocence" when filing a second or subsequent petition for *habeas* relief. Ordinarily, and indeed logically, the showing of innocence *follows*, rather than precedes, the holding of a hearing and the requirement that prosecutors open their files and evidence. A hearing gives a defendant-petitioner the ability to subpoena documents and witnesses, and to force witnesses to testify under oath. It is perverse logic that requires a petitioner to prove his or her innocence *before* obtaining these fundamental resources and due process guarantees. In fact, it is all but impossible.

Moreover, in an argument against AEDPA's one-year limitation, the *Harvard Law Review* in February 2016 suggested that this time limit might violate the suspension clause of the U.S. Constitution. Prisoners cannot be expected to put together a *habeas* petition within a year of conviction. They are dealing with the trauma of incarceration, they may not have access to counsel, or they may still be unearthing exculpatory information.† Indeed, it took legal counsel (including Sidney Powell) six years to uncover evidence the government had hidden in the Merrill Lynch–Enron case, and then it was produced to her accidentally by new government counsel.[34]

---

† As the Jeffrey MacDonald case demonstrates, it often takes more than a year to discover how agents and prosecutors have put thumbs on the scales of justice.

At a minimum, the time limit should be extended to five years, and a discovery rule added so that the government's suppression of evidence cannot deny a prisoner the right to file a writ because of the passage of time.[35]

The contributors at the *Harvard Law Review* offer a potential solution: The Supreme Court should rule that after the one-year time limit on section 2255 motions has expired, federal prisoners should be able to seek relief under 28 U.S.C. § 2241, the other, seldom-used *habeas* statute that is not curtailed under AEDPA. Currently, access to section 2241 is so limited that it is essentially defunct, but the Supreme Court has the power to revive it. Of course, the Court could simply toss out the provision of section 2255 that imposes the statute of limitations, but that kind of drastic action is unlikely. The solution offered by the *Harvard Law Review* would allow the Court to widen access to *habeas* relief without declaring anything unconstitutional. Put another way, what is needed is a solution that does not require the judiciary to say that it has been wrong all this time, or that Congress was wrong to have so shrunk the writ of *habeas corpus*. It could be an elegant solution. Practitioners should begin actively litigating this issue.

The Supreme Court should also make it easier for federal judges to overturn *state* convictions when a *habeas* petitioner's constitutional rights are clearly violated. Under the Court's current interpretation of AEDPA, federal judges are almost entirely prohibited from exercising this power. In the 2011 case *Harrington v. Richter*, the Supreme Court reversed the Ninth Circuit's decision to grant *habeas* relief to a state prisoner, holding that, under AEDPA, it's not enough for a petitioner to show that a state court's decision was incorrect; he must also show that it was "unreasonable." Specifically, the mistake must be "so lacking in justification that there was an error well understood and comprehended in existing law beyond any possibility for fair-minded disagreement."[36] In other words, to obtain *habeas* relief, state prisoners must clear an extremely high bar, as state courts are given enormous deference even when they are violating a prisoner's constitutional rights. In this decision, the Supreme Court reinforced the stranglehold that AEDPA has placed on *habeas corpus* doctrine. The Supreme Court must reverse course, unless Congress can manage to do so.

But the problems with post-conviction jurisprudence do not begin and end with AEDPA. Even if the law were repealed in its entirety, petitions for writs of *habeas corpus* and *coram nobis* would still tend to come before the original trial and/or sentencing judge. For petitioners like Conrad Black and Jeffrey MacDonald, this custom presents a serious obstacle in their quests for justice.

Post-conviction petitions warrant fresh eyes. They should, by statute, be directed to a new judge, rather than to the judge who is called upon to defend her own earlier decisions. Not only does a new set of eyes sometimes reveal some previously elusive insight, but human nature need not be challenged by the requirement that the trial judge see, and confess, the error of her ways before a *habeas* hearing can proceed. (Indeed, a strong policy argument can even be made that such hearings be held in a different geographic district altogether.)

The Supreme Court should revive the writ of *coram nobis*. As explained earlier in this chapter, most circuit courts of appeal (except for the Ninth Circuit) require a petitioner to show an "ongoing civil disability" to be eligible for *coram nobis* relief. The so-called "civil disabilities test" is far too high a bar. Because there is disagreement among the circuit courts about how to interpret *coram nobis*, the Supreme Court should hear a case challenging the legitimacy of the civil disabilities test. Of course, this requires practitioners to pursue it.

The Supreme Court should dismantle the procedural hurdle that denies many petitioners the opportunity to challenge their convictions. That court has the luxury of being able to review the cases that it wishes. Surely *habeas corpus*, long considered the most important single right in the Anglo-American legal firmament, deserves extraordinary judicial attention, and resuscitation, at the top.

Another very serious issue for current or former prisoners seeking post-conviction relief is access to legal counsel. In the landmark 1963 case *Gideon v. Wainwright,* the Supreme Court ruled that defendants in criminal trials are constitutionally entitled to an attorney, regardless of their ability to pay.[37] As a result of this decision, public defender services, funded by state and federal governments, have sprung up around the country. However, *Gideon* protections do not extend to the post-conviction stage, as the Supreme Court clarified in later decisions.[38] This is a huge obstacle to justice.

Habeas corpus law is "a dizzying maze of interrelated statutes," according to members of the venerable *Harvard Law Review,* and "AEDPA itself is a Frankenstein's monster of a law."[39] If top legal minds find this area of the law perplexing, imagine how daunting it must be for an indigent prisoner. Thomas C. O'Bryant, a Florida prisoner and self-described "jailhouse lawyer," published an extraordinary article in the *Harvard Civil Rights–Civil Liberties Law Review* inveighing against AEDPA's impact on access to *habeas corpus* relief.[40] O'Bryant discusses the formidable challenges that indigent petitioners face, and observes that "the average prisoner lacks the education, and sometimes the mental competency, necessary to pursue meaningful and timely post-conviction remedies."[41] Although public defender services are overtaxed as it is, we suggest that they take on more cases in the post-conviction stage. Federal and state governments should allocate more funds to serve this end. Protections against miscarriages of justice should remain a top priority, and our governmental budgets must demonstrate an abiding commitment to liberty and due process.

Given the myriad flaws in the criminal justice system, the law should always allow challenges to a conviction when new evidence may invalidate it. The numerous procedural obstacles that petitioners face to access writs of *habeas corpus* or *coram nobis* gut the protections our Founding Fathers tried to establish and preserve.

Unless the doors to the prison cell can be opened under reasonable conditions, the criminal justice system will continue to condemn even the demonstrably innocent to the modern equivalent of ancient dank dungeons where neither hope nor justice penetrate the darkness. And consequently, the conviction and imprisonment of the innocent will remain a closely held secret within the system that likes to boast that it is the best in the world.

ACTION ITEMS FOR CRIMINAL JUSTICE REFORM

Everyone asks: "What can I do to make things better right now—as an individual?" In this subject area, that is an especially difficult question, because many of the solutions require legislative or judicial action outside our immediate control. There are several things each of us can do, however, and our readers have taken the first step by caring enough to read this book.

WHAT CAN WE DO NOW?

1. Talk about these issues with everyone you know—at the hair salon, dinner with friends or family, anywhere you can start a conversation. The first step is making people aware and informed of the issues that create the problem.

2. Serve on a jury. U.S. District Judge William Young from Boston traveled around the country one year giving a rousing speech on the importance of the jury. One of his most important points is that the single juror is the last bastion of democracy. If a single juror votes "not guilty" on all counts

and maintains that position, she can stop an unjust conviction, because a guilty verdict requires unanimity. Jurors are supposed to use their common sense and reason. If the judge is running a railroad, the prosecution has hidden evidence, piled on charges, or engaged in some other abuse, a juror can shut it all down by maintaining a "not guilty" vote on each count. These days, conviction on a single count in federal court after a trial usually means a term of imprisonment. The only way for a juror to ensure against that is to vote "not guilty" on every count.

3. In many states, judges are elected. District attorneys are elected. Grill the district attorney candidates to adopt a firm policy for disclosure of information to the defense. Is she willing to have an open-file policy? Ask her view of *Brady*. Speak up and out! Pay attention to these elections and what the candidates propose for law enforcement. Are the judicial candidates willing to adopt a *Brady* compliance order like those we have included in the Appendices?

4. Write and call your senators and congressmen to vote for criminal justice reform. They really do respond to massive pressure from their constituents. A bill like the Fairness in Disclosure of Evidence Act should be passed, along with *mens rea* reform and the other issues we have outlined here. The current administration, atypical in its thinking in many ways, may present a rare opportunity to get meaningful criminal justice reforms enacted.

5. Remember and reinforce the presumption of innocence. We all tend to jump to a conclusion of someone's guilt as soon as we hear anything about a case. Yet our criminal justice system is in theory founded on the presumption that everyone is innocent until proven guilty beyond a reasonable doubt. As seen in the cases discussed here, a prosecutor can make anyone sound guilty even when their conduct is completely innocent. An indictment is not evidence of guilt, yet when it is read to a jury, a person is virtually convicted already. It is as

though the presumption were reversed. Add the presumption of innocence to the issues to be discussed with your friends and family.

WHAT CAN JUDGES DO?

1. Right now, today, every state and federal judge in the country could adopt a *Brady* compliance order as Judge Emmet Sullivan has done in his courtroom. This is an immediate, no-cost solution for a huge problem.
2. Right now, every state and federal judge could read this book and start holding the prosecution's feet to the fire—compelling prosecutors to meet their constitutional, legal, and ethical obligations in every case—and viewing representations by prosecutors with a healthy degree of skepticism.
3. Judges should also use more of the discretion they do have to find creative alternatives to incarceration after a conviction in circumstances where there is neither risk of flight nor danger to the community. Additionally, judges should be more willing to find that there are significant issues for appeal. Especially in complex cases encompassing novel theories of criminal liability brought by overly creative prosecutors, a defendant should not be confined until he has had his case reviewed and affirmed on appeal.
4. Judges should be more vigorous gatekeepers against indictments that are overreaching and either do not charge a crime or criminalize innocent conduct. They should also enter a judgment of acquittal at the close of the government's case when prosecutors have not come close to proving guilt beyond a reasonable doubt.

WHAT CAN CONGRESS DO?

1. Pass legislation discussed herein to codify the *Brady* rule and to set a baseline *mens rea* for all offenses.

2. Add a provision to the United States Code to make clear that only Congress can criminalize conduct. Executive branch administrative agencies do not have the power to expand or fill in statutes via regulations that propound novel theories of criminality. Concepts like conspiracy, aiding and abetting, and fraud (mail fraud, bank fraud, or wire fraud) are not totally elastic concepts that allow agencies, in effect, to create crimes by administrative action according to their whims.

3. Add a statement to 18 U.S.C. §1001 to require proof by means of a recorded statement that includes a warning of rights, so that the FBI and other law enforcement agencies can no longer stack the deck and frame people on false-statement charges by claiming the defendant made incriminating or false statements during unrecorded interrogations or interviews.

4. Restore to the district judges the discretion to allow nonviolent, first-time offenders who are no danger or risk of flight to remain on bond pending their appeals. The Merrill Lynch executives spent up to a year in prison on concocted charges because the current statute all but compels incarceration upon conviction and sentencing. Besides, a defendant who is free pretrial is better able to work with legal counsel to prepare an effective defense, and the same is true on appeal.

5. Remove absolute immunity protection from prosecutors so that they may be sued for their intentional misconduct, such as deliberately hiding evidence of innocence that results in wrongful incarceration.

6. Restore far more sentencing discretion to the district judges and take away the incentive for prosecutors to stack charges to crush their targets. Allow for far more creative alternatives to incarceration when there is neither a risk of flight nor danger to the community.

ADDITIONAL RECOMMENDATIONS

1. *Qualifications for the federal bench must be reexamined.* The president appoints all federal judges, and they serve life terms subject only to impeachment, which virtually never happens. These are extremely important and powerful positions. Federal district judges are the trial courts. There is an old joke that God wears a robe in Heaven because he thinks he is a federal judge. Federal district judges are almost monarchs in their courtrooms. They have enormous power, and great care must be taken to ensure we have judges who will be as objective, impartial, and experienced as possible.

   It is our considered opinion that no one should be appointed to the federal bench directly from a position as a prosecutor—and certainly not without several years of criminal defense experience if the nominee has ever served as a prosecutor. Depth and breadth of experience are both desperately needed on the federal bench. We would recommend that no one be appointed to a federal bench without at least twenty years of experience practicing law. To be qualified for the position of federal district judge, persons should have practiced civil and criminal law for a minimum of two decades. Not only legal experience is needed; life experience is equally important for a position that allows and often requires one to deprive people of their lives, liberties, and property. We recommend that presidents consider judicial nominees with far more diverse backgrounds in education, professional experience, and life in general.

   Our courts of appeals are the court of last resort for almost every litigant. Each person is allowed an appeal as of right to the federal court of appeals. Each year, the United States Supreme Court only hears approximately sixty cases out of the thousands in which petitions for writ of certiorari are filed. This makes federal appellate judges so important. There has been an escalating tendency by presidents from both parties to appoint younger people to these positions—on the district court and on the appellate court. This is done to extend the influence of each appointment. We would encourage the appointment of people to the appellate bench who have at least twenty-five years of experience in the active practice of law on both prosecution and defense in a wide variety of cases.

2. *Members of both houses of Congress should be subject to limits on terms in office.* Senator Ted Cruz (Texas) has introduced legislation to put term limits on United States senators and congressmen. He proposed limiting senators to two 6-year terms and representatives to three 2-year terms. One of the biggest problems in our government arises from the self-interest of those entrenched in it. We are supposed to have a citizen government—not career politicians who have never held a real job or had to meet a payroll. They become intertwined with lobbyists and other special interests, and they grow rich while the business of the country is ignored and our debt spirals out of control.

• • •

Thank you for taking the time to read this book and for considering these issues. Add your own ideas to these as we work to stop the conviction machine. One need not be a lawyer, a legislator, a judge, or a scholar to see how the system can be improved.

ACKNOWLEDGMENTS

Sidney Powell

I appreciate the assistance of my younger colleagues Molly McCann and Ben Adams, who helped with research and drafting of discrete points, and my assistant Tricia Dale, who manages to keep me on track. Of course, I can never express enough thanks to my family and my dearest friends (you know who you are) for their unending moral support and encouragement throughout this process.

I would also like to thank, especially, my co-author Harvey Silverglate, who started this book and was kind enough to invite me to join the project. His assistants Nathan McGuire and Monika Greco were also invaluable, and the team with Roger Kimball, Carol Staswick, and Amanda DeMatto at Encounter Books has been a pure pleasure in collaboration.

Harvey Silverglate

I would like first to acknowledge Matthew Power, my nephew, adventurer extraordinaire, and perhaps the finest nonfiction writer I've ever known, who died of heatstroke tragically young while on assignment in Uganda reporting on an exploration of the Nile.

Next, I must acknowledge my extraordinary co-author Sidney Powell, who jumped into this project at a busy time for her and helped bring it to fruition.

In addition, my thanks to many people who have been helpful to my work: Sam Abady, Jeanne Baker, Ed Bartlett, Zachary Bloom, Nancy Bruett, Rob Cary, Miriam Conrad, Howard Cooper, Rachel Davidson, Amanda DeMatto, Aaron Voloj Dessauer,

Juliana DeVries, Elsa Dorfman, David Duncan, Otto Eckstein, Cathy Fleming, Monika Greco, Wendy Kaminer, Elizabeth Kelley, Roger Kimball, Adam Kissel, Dustin Lewis, Alana Massie, Nathan McGuire, Daniel Medwed, Randal John Meyer, Samantha Miller, Judith Mizner, Timothy Moore, Frank Quattrone, Thane Ritchie, Barry Scheck, Daniel Schneider, Michael Schneider, Daniel Schwartz, Daniel Shuchman, Ahron Singer, Jo Stafford, Carol Staswick, Beth Stewart, Thomas P. Sullivan, James F. Tierney, Andrew W. Vail, Martin Weinberg, Jan Wolfe, Norman Zalkind.

APPENDICES

A. Federal Bureau of Investigation Policy on Electronic Recording of Confessions and Witness Interviews

B. Federal Rules of Criminal Procedure: Rule 6. The Grand Jury

C. North Carolina General Statutes: § 15A-903. Disclosure of evidence by the State—Information subject to disclosure

D. Standing *Brady* Order, Judge Emmet G. Sullivan

E. Draft of Standing *Brady* Order, Sidney Powell

A. Federal Bureau of Investigation Policy on Electronic Recording of Confessions and Witness Interviews

(Rev. 01-31-2003)

FEDERAL BUREAU OF INVESTIGATION

Precedence: ROUTINE   Date: 3/23/2006

To: All Field Offices   Attn: ADIC, SAC, and CDC
     All HQ Divisions   EAD; AD
                                       FBIHQ, Manuals Desk
     All Legats   Legal Attache

From: Office of the General Counsel
       Investigative Law Unit
       Contact: Jung-Won Choi (202)324-9625

Approved By: Caproni Valerie E
              Lammert Elaine N
              Larson David C

Drafted By: Choi Jung-Won

Case ID #: 66F-HQ-1283488-3
            66F-HQ-C1384970

Title: ELECTRONIC RECORDING OF CONFESSIONS AND WITNESS
        INTERVIEWS

Synopsis: To clarify existing FBI policy on electronic recording
of confessions and to provide guidance on some of the factors
that the SAC should consider when deciding whether to authorize
recording.

Administrative: This document is a privileged FBI attorney
communication and may not be disseminated outside the FBI without
OGC approval. To read the footnotes in this document, it may be
required to download and print the document in WordPerfect.

Details: FBI policy on electronic recording of confessions and
witness interviews is contained in SAC Memorandum 22-99, dated 10
August 1999, which revised SAC Memorandum 22-98, dated 24 July
1998. Under the current policy, agents may not electronically
record confessions or interviews, openly or surreptitiously,
unless authorized by the SAC or his or her designee. See MIOG,
Part II, Section 10-10.10(2). Consultation with an AUSA, CDC, or
OGC may be appropriate in certain circumstances, but it is not
required.[1] In certain circumstances (set forth in the above)

---

[1] If the recording is going to be surreptitious, SACs are urged to
obtain the concurrence of the CDC or the appropriate OGC attorney. In
addition, in accordance with the Attorney General's "Procedure for Lawful,
Warrantless Monitoring of Verbal Communication," dated May 30, 2002, advice
that the proposed surreptitious recording is both legal and appropriate must
be obtained from the USA, AUSA or DOJ attorney responsible for the
investigation.

To: All Field Offices From: Office of the General Counsel
Re: 66F-HQ-1283488-3, 3/23/2006

guidance),[2] FBIHQ concurrence is required.

In recent years, there has been on-going debate in the criminal justice community whether to make electronic recording of custodial interrogations mandatory. According to a study published in 2004 by a former U.S. Attorney,[3] 238 law enforcement agencies in 37 states and the District of Columbia electronically record some or all custodial interviews of suspects. In four of those jurisdictions, electronic recording is mandated by law - by legislation in Illinois and the District of Columbia and by case law opinions issued by the state supreme courts of Alaska and Minnesota. In addition, it is the practice in some foreign countries--such as Great Britain and Australia--to record all interviews of suspects, and some U.S. Attorneys feel strongly that at least some interviews should be required to be recorded.[4]

There is no federal law that requires federal agents to electronically record custodial interviews and, to our knowledge, no federal law enforcement agency currently mandates this practice. There have been isolated incidents in which federal district court judges, as well as some United States Attorneys, have urged the FBI to revise its current policy to require recording all custodial interviews, or at least those involving selected serious offenses. In addition, agents testifying to statements made by criminal defendants have increasingly faced intense cross-examination concerning this policy in apparent efforts to cast doubt upon the voluntariness of statements in the absence of recordings or the accuracy of the testimony regarding the content of the statement. Furthermore, in some task force cases that result in state prosecution, FBI state or local partners have been precluded from using FBI agent testimony of the defendant's confession because of restrictive state law or policy.

---

[2] These circumstances include, among other things, extensive media scrutiny, difficult legal issues, complex operational concerns, or significant involvement by FBIHQ.

[3] Thomas P. Sullivan, *Police Experiences with Recording Custodial Interrogations*, Northwestern University School of Law, Center on Wrongful Convictions, Number 1, Summer 2004.

[4] There is a group within the Department of Justice, which includes the FBI, DEA, ATF and the Marshals Service, that has met periodically to discuss this issue. It is conceivable that an outgrowth of those discussions will be a pilot program in one or more judicial districts in which recording at least certain interviews will be required.

2

To: All Field Offices From: Office of the General Counsel
Re: 66F-HQ-1283488-3, 3/23/2006

Against this backdrop, FBI executive management has reviewed the current policy. After a careful deliberation of all the available options, the Director has opted for now to retain the current policy but has tasked the General Counsel to issue guidance on the factors that the SAC or his or her designee should consider before granting exceptions.

Before listing those factors, a brief review of the sound reasons behind the FBI policy on electronic recording of confessions and interviews is in order. First, the presence of recording equipment may interfere with and undermine the successful rapport-building interviewing technique which the FBI practices.[5] Second, FBI agents have successfully testified to custodial defendants' statements for generations with only occasional, and rarely successful, challenges. Third, as all experienced investigators and prosecutors know, perfectly lawful and acceptable interviewing techniques do not always come across in recorded fashion to lay persons as proper means of obtaining information from defendants. Initial resistance may be interpreted as involuntariness and misleading a defendant as to the quality of the evidence against him may appear to be unfair deceit. Finally, there are 56 fields offices and over 400 resident agencies in the FBI. A requirement to record all custodial interviews throughout the agency would not only involve massive logistic and transcription support but would also create unnecessary obstacles to the admissibility of lawfully obtained statements, which through inadvertence or circumstances beyond control of the interviewing agents, could not be recorded.

Notwithstanding these reasons for not mandating recording, it is recognized that there are many situations in which recording a subject's interview would be prudent. For this reason, it has been FBI policy for nearly eight years to grant an SAC the authority and flexibility to permit recording if he or she deems it advisable.

Often, during the time this policy has been in effect, SAC discretion has been viewed negatively; i.e., as an "exception" to the "no recording" policy, instead of positively; i.e., as a case-by-case opportunity to use this technique where and when it will further the investigation and the subsequent prosecution. Supervisors are encouraged to seek permission to record, and SACs are encouraged to grant it, whenever it is determined that these objectives will be met.

---

[5] In theory, surreptitious recording would not affect this approach. However, if recording became routine practice, it would not take long before that practice became well known—especially among members of organized crime.

3

To: All Field Offices From: Office of the General Counsel
Re: 66F-HQ-1283488-3, 3/23/2006

When deciding whether to exercise this discretion, SACs are encouraged to consider the following factors:

1) Whether the purpose of the interview is to gather evidence for prosecution, or intelligence for analysis, or both;

2) If prosecution is anticipated, the type and seriousness of the crime, including, in particular, whether the crime has a mental element (such as knowledge or intent to defraud), proof of which would be considerably aided by the defendant's admissions in his own words;

3) Whether the defendant's own words and appearance (in video recordings) would help rebut any doubt about the voluntariness of his confession raised by his age, mental state, educational level, or understanding of the English language; or is otherwise expected to be an issue at trial, such as to rebut an insanity defense; or may be of value to behavioral analysts;

4) The sufficiency of other available evidence to prove the charge beyond a reasonable doubt;

5) The preference of the United States Attorney's Office and the Federal District Court regarding recorded confessions;

6) Local laws and practice--particularly in task force investigations where state prosecution is possible;

7) Whether interviews with other subjects in the same or related cases have been electronically recorded;

8) The potential to use the subject as a cooperating witness and the value of using his own words to elicit his cooperation;

9) Practical considerations--such as the expected length of the interview; the availability of recording equipment and transcription (and, if necessary, translation) services; and the time and available resources required to obtain them. If cost factors prove prohibitive, consider whether the requesting U.S. Attorney's Office will agree to pay for the services.

These factors should not be viewed as a checklist and are not intended to limit the SAC's discretion. It is recognized, however, that establishing reasonable standards on the type of cases, crimes, circumstances, and subjects for which recording is a desirable objective so as to maintain internal field office consistency and to inform field agents and supervisors when and why to request recording.

4

DAG000001630

To: All Field Offices . From: Office of the General Counsel
Re: 66F-HQ-1283488-3, 3/23/2006

      Field office standards are to be encouraged for another
very important reason.   The absence of any standard by which
field office discretion in this matter is exercised will render
testifying agents vulnerable to attack on cross-examination.   If,
on the other hand, an agent can point to identifiable standards
that provide a reasonable explanation for why some interviews are
recorded and others are not, the implication that the agent chose
not to record an interview to mask the involuntary nature of the
defendant's admissions will be much harder to argue.[6]   This office
is prepared to assist in the preparation of such standards if
desired.

      Finally, in order to assist agents who testify to
unrecorded admissions, an explanation of this policy and the
reasons behind it should be added to field office quarterly legal
training.   Questions may be directed to Assistant General Counsel
Jung-Won Choi, at the Office of the General Counsel,
Investigative Law Unit, at 202-324-9625.

---

  [6] Carrying this point further, it would be even easier to withstand
cross-examination if a fixed policy as to when to record and when not to
record were established at FBI Headquarters that permits no field office or
agent discretion.   Yet, such an advantage would be far off set by the loss of
flexibility that field office SACs and supervisors need to make sound
investigative decisions such as the choice of interviewing techniques.

To: All Field Offices From: Office of the General Counsel
Re: 66F-HQ-1283488-3, 3/23/2006

LEAD(s):

Set Lead 1: (Action)

   ALL RECEIVING OFFICES

        Disseminate to all personnel. The CDC of each field
office should be the principal point of contact for this EC and
should provide a briefing to the agents in his or her office
consistent with this EC.

◆◆

1 - Ms. Caproni
1 - Mr. Kelley
1 - Ms. Gulyassy
1 - Ms. Thomas
1 - Ms. Lammert
1 - Mr. Larson
1 - Mr. Choi
2 - ILU

6

(March 23, 2006) http://www.nytimes.com/
packages/pdf/national/20070402_FBI_Memo.pdf

B. Federal Rules of Criminal Procedure
Rule 6. The Grand Jury

(a) Summoning a Grand Jury.

   (1) *In General.* When the public interest so requires, the court must order that one or more grand juries be summoned. A grand jury must have 16 to 23 members, and the court must order that enough legally qualified persons be summoned to meet this requirement.

   (2) *Alternate Jurors.* When a grand jury is selected, the court may also select alternate jurors. Alternate jurors must have the same qualifications and be selected in the same manner as any other juror. Alternate jurors replace jurors in the same sequence in which the alternates were selected. An alternate juror who replaces a juror is subject to the same challenges, takes the same oath, and has the same authority as the other jurors.

(b) Objection to the Grand Jury or to a Grand Juror.

   (1) *Challenges.* Either the government or a defendant may challenge the grand jury on the ground that it was not lawfully drawn, summoned, or selected, and may challenge an individual juror on the ground that the juror is not legally qualified.

   (2) *Motion to Dismiss an Indictment.* A party may move to dismiss the indictment based on an objection to the grand jury or on an individual juror's lack of legal qualification, unless the court has previously ruled on the same objection under Rule 6(b)(1). The motion to dismiss is governed by 28 U.S.C. § 1867(e). The court must not dismiss the indictment on the ground that a grand juror was not legally qualified if the record shows that at least 12 qualified jurors concurred in the indictment.

(c) Foreperson and Deputy Foreperson. The court will appoint one juror as the foreperson and another as the deputy foreperson. In the foreperson's absence, the deputy foreperson will act as the foreperson. The foreperson may administer oaths and affirmations and will sign all indictments. The foreperson—or another juror designated by the foreperson—will record the number of jurors concurring in every indictment and will file the record with the clerk, but the record may not be made public unless the court so orders.

(d) Who May Be Present.

   (1) *While the Grand Jury Is in Session.* The following persons may be present while the grand jury is in session: attorneys for the government, the witness being questioned, interpreters when needed, and a court reporter or an operator of a recording device.

   (2) *During Deliberations and Voting.* No person other than the jurors, and any interpreter needed to assist a hearing-impaired or speech-impaired juror, may be present while the grand jury is deliberating or voting.

(e) Recording and Disclosing the Proceedings.

   (1) *Recording the Proceedings.* Except while the grand jury is deliberating or voting, all proceedings must be recorded by a court reporter or by a suitable recording device. But the validity of a prosecution is not affected by the unintentional failure to make a recording. Unless the court orders otherwise, an attorney for the government will retain control of the recording, the reporter's notes, and any transcript prepared from those notes.

   (2) *Secrecy.*

      (A) No obligation of secrecy may be imposed on any person except in accordance with Rule 6(e)(2)(B).

(B) Unless these rules provide otherwise, the following persons must not disclose a matter occurring before the grand jury:

    (i) a grand juror;

    (ii) an interpreter;

    (iii) a court reporter;

    (iv) an operator of a recording device;

    (v) a person who transcribes recorded testimony;

    (vi) an attorney for the government; or

    (vii) a person to whom disclosure is made under Rule 6(e)(3)(A)(ii) or (iii).

(3) *Exceptions.*

(A) Disclosure of a grand-jury matter—other than the grand jury's deliberations or any grand juror's vote—may be made to:

    (i) an attorney for the government for use in performing that attorney's duty;

    (ii) any government personnel—including those of a state, state subdivision, Indian tribe, or foreign government—that an attorney for the government considers necessary to assist in performing that attorney's duty to enforce federal criminal law; or

    (iii) a person authorized by 18 U.S.C. § 3322.

(B) A person to whom information is disclosed under Rule 6(e)(3)(A)(ii) may use that information only to assist an attorney for the government in performing that attorney's duty to enforce federal criminal law. An attorney for the government must promptly provide the court that impaneled the grand jury with the names of all persons to whom a disclosure has been made, and must certify that the attorney has advised those persons of their obligation of secrecy under this rule.

(C) An attorney for the government may disclose any grand-jury matter to another federal grand jury.

(D) An attorney for the government may disclose any grand-jury matter involving foreign intelligence, counterintelligence (as defined in 50 U.S.C. § 3003), or foreign intelligence information (as defined in Rule 6(e)(3)(D)(iii)) to any federal law enforcement, intelligence, protective, immigration, national defense, or national security official to assist the official receiving the information in the performance of that official's duties. An attorney for the government may also disclose any grand-jury matter involving, within the United States or elsewhere, a threat of attack or other grave hostile acts of a foreign power or its agent, a threat of domestic or international sabotage or terrorism, or clandestine intelligence gathering activities by an intelligence service or network of a foreign power or by its agent, to any appropriate federal, state, state subdivision, Indian tribal, or foreign government official, for the purpose of preventing or responding to such threat or activities.

   (i) Any official who receives information under Rule 6(e)(3)(D) may use the information only as necessary in the conduct of that person's official duties subject to any limitations on the unauthorized disclosure of such information. Any state, state subdivision, Indian tribal, or foreign government official who receives information under Rule 6(e)(3)(D) may use the information only in a manner consistent with any guidelines issued by the Attorney General and the Director of National Intelligence.

(ii) Within a reasonable time after disclosure is made under Rule 6(e)(3)(D), an attorney for the government must file, under seal, a notice with the court in the district where the grand jury convened stating that such information was disclosed and the departments, agencies, or entities to which the disclosure was made.

(iii) As used in Rule 6(e)(3)(D), the term "foreign intelligence information" means:

(a) information, whether or not it concerns a United States person, that relates to the ability of the United States to protect against—

- actual or potential attack or other grave hostile acts of a foreign power or its agent;
- sabotage or international terrorism by a foreign power or its agent; or
- clandestine intelligence activities by an intelligence service or network of a foreign power or by its agent; or

(b) information, whether or not it concerns a United States person, with respect to a foreign power or foreign territory that relates to—

- the national defense or the security of the United States; or

- the conduct of the foreign affairs of the United States.

(E) The court may authorize disclosure—at a time, in a manner, and subject to any other conditions that it directs—of a grand-jury matter:

   (i) preliminarily to or in connection with a judicial proceeding;

   (ii) at the request of a defendant who shows that a ground may exist to dismiss the indictment because of a matter that occurred before the grand jury;

   (iii) at the request of the government, when sought by a foreign court or prosecutor for use in an official criminal investigation;

   (iv) at the request of the government if it shows that the matter may disclose a violation of State, Indian tribal, or foreign criminal law, as long as the disclosure is to an appropriate state, state-subdivision, Indian tribal, or foreign government official for the purpose of enforcing that law; or

   (v) at the request of the government if it shows that the matter may disclose a violation of military criminal law under the Uniform Code of Military Justice, as long as the disclosure is to an appropriate military official for the purpose of enforcing that law.

(F) A petition to disclose a grand-jury matter under Rule 6(e)(3)(E)(i) must be filed in the district where the grand jury convened. Unless the hearing is ex parte—as it may be when the government is the petitioner—the petitioner must serve the petition on, and the court must afford a reasonable opportunity to appear and be heard to:

    (i)   an attorney for the government;

    (ii)   the parties to the judicial proceeding; and

    (iii)   any other person whom the court may designate.

(G) If the petition to disclose arises out of a judicial proceeding in another district, the petitioned court must transfer the petition to the other court unless the petitioned court can reasonably determine whether disclosure is proper. If the petitioned court decides to transfer, it must send to the transferee court the material sought to be disclosed, if feasible, and a written evaluation of the need for continued grand-jury secrecy. The transferee court must afford those persons identified in Rule 6(e)(3)(F) a reasonable opportunity to appear and be heard.

(4) *Sealed Indictment.* The magistrate judge to whom an indictment is returned may direct that the indictment be kept secret until the defendant is in custody or has been released pending trial. The clerk must then seal the indictment, and no person may disclose the indictment's existence except as necessary to issue or execute a warrant or summons.

(5) *Closed Hearing.* Subject to any right to an open hearing in a contempt proceeding, the court must close any hearing to the extent necessary to prevent disclosure of a matter occurring before a grand jury.

(6) *Sealed Records.* Records, orders, and subpoenas relating to grand-jury proceedings must be kept under seal to the extent and as long as necessary to prevent

the unauthorized disclosure of a matter occurring before a grand jury.

(7) *Contempt.* A knowing violation of Rule 6, or of any guidelines jointly issued by the Attorney General and the Director of National Intelligence under Rule 6, may be punished as a contempt of court.

(f) Indictment and Return. A grand jury may indict only if at least 12 jurors concur. The grand jury—or its foreperson or deputy foreperson—must return the indictment to a magistrate judge in open court. To avoid unnecessary cost or delay, the magistrate judge may take the return by video teleconference from the court where the grand jury sits. If a complaint or information is pending against the defendant and 12 jurors do not concur in the indictment, the foreperson must promptly and in writing report the lack of concurrence to the magistrate judge.

(g) Discharging the Grand Jury. A grand jury must serve until the court discharges it, but it may serve more than 18 months only if the court, having determined that an extension is in the public interest, extends the grand jury's service. An extension may be granted for no more than 6 months, except as otherwise provided by statute.

(h) Excusing a Juror. At any time, for good cause, the court may excuse a juror either temporarily or permanently, and if permanently, the court may impanel an alternate juror in place of the excused juror.

(i) "Indian Tribe" Defined. "Indian tribe" means an Indian tribe recognized by the Secretary of the Interior on a list published in the Federal Register under 25 U.S.C. § 479a–1.

Source: Legal Information Institute, Cornell Law School, https://www.law.cornell.edu/rules/frcrmp/rule_6

C. North Carolina General Statutes § 15A-903
Disclosure of evidence by the State—Information
subject to disclosure

(a) Upon motion of the defendant, the court must order:

(1) The State to make available to the defendant the complete files of all law enforcement agencies, investigatory agencies, and prosecutors' offices involved in the investigation of the crimes committed or the prosecution of the defendant.

a. The term "file" includes the defendant's statements, the codefendants' statements, witness statements, investigating officers' notes, results of tests and examinations, or any other matter or evidence obtained during the investigation of the offenses alleged to have been committed by the defendant. When any matter or evidence is submitted for testing or examination, in addition to any test or examination results, all other data, calculations, or writings of any kind shall be made available to the defendant, including, but not limited to, preliminary test or screening results and bench notes.

b. The term "prosecutor's office" refers to the office of the prosecuting attorney.

b1. The term "investigatory agency" includes any public or private entity that obtains information on behalf of a law enforcement agency or prosecutor's office in connection with the investigation of the crimes committed or the prosecution of the defendant.

c. Oral statements shall be in written or recorded form, except that oral statements made by a witness to a prosecuting attorney outside the presence of a law enforcement officer or investigatorial assistant shall not be required to be in written or recorded form unless there is significantly new or different information in the oral statement from a prior statement made by the witness.

    d. The defendant shall have the right to inspect and copy or photograph any materials contained therein and, under appropriate safeguards, to inspect, examine, and test any physical evidence or sample contained therein.

(2) The prosecuting attorney to give notice to the defendant of any expert witnesses that the State reasonably expects to call as a witness at trial. Each such witness shall prepare, and the State shall furnish to the defendant, a report of the results of any examinations or tests conducted by the expert. The State shall also furnish to the defendant the expert's curriculum vitae, the expert's opinion, and the underlying basis for that opinion. The State shall give the notice and furnish the materials required by this subsection within a reasonable time prior to trial, as specified by the court. Standardized fee scales shall be developed by the Administrative Office of the Courts and Indigent Defense Services for all expert witnesses and private investigators who are compensated with State funds.

(3) The prosecuting attorney to give the defendant, at the beginning of jury selection, a written list of the names of all other witnesses whom the State reasonably expects to call during the trial. Names of witnesses shall not be subject to disclosure if the prosecuting attorney certifies in writing and under seal to the court

that to do so may subject the witnesses or others to physical or substantial economic harm or coercion, or that there is other particularized, compelling need not to disclose. If there are witnesses that the State did not reasonably expect to call at the time of the provision of the witness list, and as a result are not listed, the court upon a good faith showing shall allow the witnesses to be called. Additionally, in the interest of justice, the court may in its discretion permit any undisclosed witness to testify.

(b) If the State voluntarily provides disclosure under G.S. 15A-902(a), the disclosure shall be to the same extent as required by subsection (a) of this section.

(c) On a timely basis, law enforcement and investigatory agencies shall make available to the prosecutor's office a complete copy of the complete files related to the investigation of the crimes committed or the prosecution of the defendant for compliance with this section and any disclosure under G.S. 15A-902(a). Investigatory agencies that obtain information and materials listed in subdivision (1) of subsection (a) of this section shall ensure that such information and materials are fully disclosed to the prosecutor's office on a timely basis for disclosure to the defendant.

(d) Any person who willfully omits or misrepresents evidence or information required to be disclosed pursuant to subdivision (1) of subsection (a) of this section, or required to be provided to the prosecutor's office pursuant to subsection (c) of this section, shall be guilty of a Class H felony. Any person who willfully omits or misrepresents evidence or information required to be disclosed pursuant to any other provision of this section shall be guilty of a Class 1 misdemeanor. (1973, c. 1286, s. 1; 1975, c. 166, s. 27; 1983, c. 759, ss. 1-3; 1983, Ex. Sess., c. 6, s. 1; 2001-282, s. 5;

2004-154, s. 4; 2007-183, s. 1; 2007-377, s. 1; 2007-393, s. 1; 2011-19, s. 9; 2011-250, s. 1.)

(Last modified: March 23, 2014)
https://law.onecle.com/north-carolina/
15a-criminal-procedure-act/15a-903.html

D. Standing *Brady* Order,
Judge Emmet G. Sullivan

UNITED STATES DISTRICT COURT
FOR THE DISTRICT OF COLUMBIA

UNITED STATES OF AMERICA,)
)
)
)
            v.   )   Criminal No. XX-XX (EGS)
)
[PARTY NAME],   )
)
            Defendant.   )
_____)

ORDER

Pursuant to *Brady v. Maryland*, 373 U.S. 83 (1963), and its progeny, the government has a continuing obligation to produce all evidence required by the law and the Federal Rules of Criminal Procedure. *See id.*, 373 U.S. at 87 (holding that due process requires disclosure of "evidence [that] is material either to guilt or to punishment" upon request); *Kyles v. Whitley*, 514 U.S. 419, 437-38 (1995) (holding that the obligation to disclose includes producing evidence "known only to police investigators and not to the prosecutor" and that "the individual prosecutor has a duty to learn of any favorable evidence known to others acting on the government's behalf . . . , including the police"); *United States v. Agurs*, 427 U.S. 97, 107 (1976) (holding that the duty to disclose exculpatory evidence applies even when there has been no request by the accused); *Giglio v. United States*, 405 U.S. 150, 153-55 (1972)

1

(holding that *Brady* encompasses impeachment evidence); *see also* Fed. R. Crim. P. 16(a) (outlining information subject to government disclosure); *United States v. Marshall*, 132 F.3d 63, 67-68 (D.C. Cir. 1998) (holding that the disclosure requirements of Federal Rule of Criminal Procedure 16(a)(1)(C) apply to inculpatory, as well as exculpatory, evidence).

The government's *Brady* obligation to provide exculpatory evidence in a timely manner is not diminished by the fact that such evidence also constitutes evidence that must be produced later pursuant to the Jencks Act, 18 U.S.C. § 3500, or by the fact that such evidence need not be produced according to Rule 16. *See United States v. Tarantino*, 846 F.2d 1384, 1414 n.11 (D.C. Cir. 1988); *see also* Advisory Committee Note to Fed. R. Crim. P. 16 (1974) ("The rule is intended to prescribe the minimum amount of discovery to which the parties are entitled."). Where doubt exists as to the usefulness of the evidence to the defendant, the government must resolve all such doubts in favor of full disclosure. *See United States v. Paxson*, 861 F.2d 730, 737 (D.C. Cir. 1988).

Accordingly, the Court, *sua sponte,* directs the government to produce to defendant in a timely manner any evidence in its possession that is favorable to defendant and material either to defendant's guilt or punishment. This government responsibility includes producing, during plea negotiations, any exculpatory

2

evidence in the government's possession.[1] The government is

further directed to produce all discoverable evidence in a

readily usable form. For example, the government must produce

documents as they are kept in the usual course of business or

must organize and label them clearly. The government must also

produce electronically-stored information in a form in which it

is ordinarily maintained unless the form is not readily usable,

in which case the government is directed to produce it in a

readily-usable form. If the information already exists or was

memorialized in a tangible format, such as a document or

---

[1]*See United States v. Ruiz*, 536 U.S. 622, 633 (2002)(government not required "to disclose material impeachment evidence prior to entering a plea agreement with a criminal defendant"); *United States v. Moussaoui*, 591 F.3d 263, 286 (4th Cir. 2010)(noting that the "Supreme Court has not addressed the question of whether the *Brady* right to *exculpatory* information, in contrast to *impeachment* information, might be extended to the guilty plea context")(emphases in the original); *United States v. Ohiri*, 133 F. App'x 555, 562 (10th Cir. 2005)("By holding in *Ruiz* that the government committed no due process violation by requiring a defendant to waive her right to impeachment evidence before indictment in order to accept a fast-track plea, the Supreme Court did not imply that the government may avoid the consequence of a *Brady* violation if the defendant accepts an eleventh-hour plea agreement while ignorant of withheld exculpatory evidence in the government's possession."); *McCann v. Mangialardi*, 337 F.3d 782, 788 (7th Cir. 2003)(noting that "given th[e significant distinction between impeachment information and exculpatory evidence of actual innocence], it is highly likely that the Supreme Court would find a violation of the Due Process Clause if prosecutors or other relevant government actors have knowledge of a criminal defendant's factual innocence but fail to disclose such information to a defendant before he enters into a guilty plea"); *United States v. Nelson*, 979 F. Supp. 2d 123, 135-36 (D.D.C. 2013)("Because the prosecution suppressed exculpatory evidence before Nelson pled guilty, Nelson's due process rights were violated to his prejudice and his guilty plea was not voluntary and knowing."); *Buffey v. Ballard*, 782 S.E.2d 204, 221 (W. Va. 2015)(finding "that the DNA results were favorable, suppressed, and material to the defense," and therefore "the Petitioner's due process rights, as enunciated in *Brady*, were violated by the State's suppression of that exculpatory evidence"). *But see United States v. Conroy*, 567 F.3d 174, 179 (5th Cir. 2009)(disagreeing with the proposition that, based on *Ruiz*, "exculpatory evidence is different [from impeachment information] and must be turned over before entry of a plea").

3

recording, the information shall be produced in that format. If the information does not exist in such a format and, as a result, the government is providing the information in a summary format, the summary must include sufficient detail and specificity to enable the defense to assess its relevance and potential usefulness.

Finally, if the government has identified any information which is favorable to the defendant but which the government believes not to be material, the government shall submit such information to the Court for *in camera* review.

SO ORDERED.

Signed: **Emmet G. Sullivan**
            United States District Judge
            Month Day, Year

4

https://www.dcd.uscourts.gov/sites/dcd/files/
StandingBradyOrder_November2017.pdf

E. Draft of Standing *Brady* Order,
Sidney Powell

IN THE UNITED STATES DISTRICT COURT
FOR THE _____

UNITED STATES OF AMERICA,
 	
    Plaintiff,
 	
v.
 	
[DEFENDANT'S NAME],
 	
    Defendant.
	)
	)
	)
	) Criminal No. _____
	)
	)
	)
	) ORDER
	)
	)
	)
	)

ORDER

Pursuant to *Brady v. Maryland*, 373 U.S. 83 (1963), and its progeny, the government has a continuing obligation to produce all evidence required by the law and the Federal Rules of Criminal Procedure. *See id.* at 87 (due process requires disclosure of "evidence [that] is material either to guilt or to punishment" upon request); *Kyles v. Whitley*, 514 U.S. 419, 437-38 (1995) (the obligation to disclose includes evidence "known only to police investigators and not to the prosecutor," and that "the individual prosecutor has a duty to learn of any favorable evidence known to others acting on the government's behalf ..., including the police."); *United States v. Agurs*, 427 U.S. 97, 107 (1976) (the duty to disclose exculpatory evidence applies even when there has been no request by the accused); *Giglio v. United States*, 405 U.S. 150, 153-54 (1972) (*Brady* encompasses impeachment evidence); *see also* FED. R. CRIM. P. 16(a) (outlining information subject to government disclosure).

Evidence that qualifies under both *Brady* and the Jencks Act shall be deemed *Brady* material and produced forthwith accordingly. The government's obligation to provide exculpatory evidence pursuant to *Brady* in a timely manner is not diminished either by the fact that such evidence also constitutes evidence that must be produced later pursuant to the Jencks Act, 18 U.S.C. § 3500, or by the fact that such evidence need not be produced according to Rule 16. *See* Advisory

1

Committee Note to FED. R. CRIM. P. 16 (1974) ("The rule is intended to prescribe the minimum amount of discovery to which the parties are entitled.").

Where doubt exists as to the usefulness of the evidence to the defendant, the government must resolve all such doubts in favor of full disclosure. *See United States v. Paxson*, 861 F.2d 730, 737 (D.C. Cir. 1988); *United States v. Starusko*, 729 F.2d 256, 263 (3d Cir. 1984).

Accordingly, the Court, *sua sponte,* directs the government to produce to defendant within fourteen days from issuance of this Order any and all evidence that is favorable to the defense either to defendant's guilt or punishment including that which tends to impeach any government witnesses. Further, the production requirement of this order repeats every 21 days and continues throughout the appellate process as any new evidence appears from any source. *Strickler v. Greene*, 527 U.S. 263, 281, 119 S.Ct. 1936, 1948 (1999).

This mandates includes all discoverable evidence and information in the possession, custody, or control of the government, the existence of which is known or may be obtained, or by the exercise of due diligence may become known or obtained. Government attorneys' own notes and those of all its agents and officers are also included and must be reviewed by government counsel in compliance with this order. This discoverable evidence and information must be produced regardless of whether it would meet the appellate materiality standard.

The government is further directed to produce all discoverable evidence in a readily usable form. For example, the government must produce documents as they are kept in the usual course of business or must organize and label them clearly. The government must also produce electronically stored information in a form in which it is ordinarily maintained unless the form is not readily usable, in which case the government is directed to produce it in a readily usable form. If the information already exists or was memorialized in a tangible format, such as a document or recording, the information shall be produced in that format.

The court requires production of actual transcripts, FBI 302s, raw notes and other actual, original documents unless the government establishes a need for those documents or the identity of specific persons to be protected. *United States v. Brown*, 303 F.3d 582, 593 (5th Cir. 2002), *cert. denied*, 537 U.S. 1173, 123 S. Ct. 1003 (2003); *Williams v. Whitley*, 940 F.2d 132, 133 (5th Cir. 1991);

Conley v. United States, 415 F.3d 183, 188-89 (1st Cir. 2005); *United States v. Harrison*, 524 F.2d 421, 427 (D.C. Cir. 1975).

A summary may be provided only with the approval of the court. A summary must include sufficient detail and specificity to enable the defense to assess its relevance and potential usefulness. In any case in which a summary is used, the underlying materials from which that summary was created must be submitted to this Court for in camera review along with the proposed summary.

The Court strongly discourages the use of summaries, and government counsel is hereby on notice that any information not produced to the court and omitted from a summary may be considered an intentional violation of *Brady* and shall be punished accordingly.

Any violation of this order may be punished by contempt of Court or any other sanctions the Court deems appropriate, including but not limited to: being barred from practice before this Court; being barred from practice within this District; being referred to the bar association for disciplinary review; being named in an opinion of this Court; being fined; and/or being referred for investigation and criminal prosecution. *Bank of Nova Scotia v. United States*, 487 U.S. 250, 263, 108 S.Ct. 2369, 2378 (1988); 18 U.S.C. § 401.

In the event of a finding that this Order has been violated, this Court may also sanction the United States by precluding the government from introducing particular evidence, granting a mis-trial or new trial, and dismissing an indictment with or without prejudice. *United States v. Hasting*, 461 U.S. 499, 505, 103 S.Ct. 1974, 1978 (1983); *Brady*, 373 U.S. at 87, 83 S. Ct. at 1197; *see also United States v. Chapman*, 524 F.3d 1073 (9th Cir. 2008), *Gov't of the Virgin Islands v. Fahie*, 419 F.3d 249 (3d Cir. 2005); *United States v. Shaffer Equipment Co.*, 11 F.3d 450 (4th Cir. 1993); *United States v. Kojayan*, 8 F.3d 1315, 1325 (9th Cir.1993).

SO ORDERED this ___ day of _____, 2014.

_____

UNITED STATES DISTRICT JUDGE

3

NOTES

PREFACE

1 Sidney Powell, *Licensed to Lie: Exposing Corruption in the Department of Justice* (2014).

2 Robert H. Jackson, "The Federal Prosecutor," April 1, 1940, delivered at the 2nd Annual Conference of United States Attorneys, in Washington, D.C., reproduced in *Journal of Criminal Law and Criminology*, vol. 31, no. 1 (May/June 1940): 3–6; and in *Journal of the American Judicature Society*, vol. 24 (June 1940): 18–20.

3 Harvey Silverglate, *Three Felonies a Day: How the Feds Target the Innocent*, 2nd ed. (New York: Encounter Books, 2011). Robert H. Jackson's famous speech to his prosecutorial assistants is discussed on pp. xxxv–xxxvi.

4 Tim Henderson, "Felony Conviction Rates Have Risen Sharply, But Unevenly," Pew Charitable Trusts, January 2, 2018; S.K.S. Shannon et al., "The Growth, Scope, and Spatial Distribution of People With Felony Records in the United States, 1948–2010," *Demography*, vol. 54, no. 5 (October 2017): 1795–1818; Matthew Friedman, "Just Facts: As Many Americans Have Criminal Records as College Diplomas," Brennan Center for Justice, November 17, 2015.

5 Shannon et al., "The Growth, Scope, and Spatial Distribution of People With Felony Records in the United States, 1948–2010."

6 Bernard Kerik, *From Jailer to Jailed: My Journey from Correction and Police Commissioner to Inmate #84888-054* (New York: Threshold Editions, 2015), 28.

7 To get a sense of the Innocence Project's important work of freeing wrongfully convicted prisoners, see www.InnocenceProject.org.

8 Powell, *Licensed to Lie*, 192–95.

9 *United States v. Stevens*, No. 08-cr-231-EGS (D.D.C. Jan. 26, 2009), Senator Stevens's Motion to Dismiss the Indictment, https://cdn.licensedtolie.com/wp-content/uploads/StevensFilingJoyComplaint.10.pdf.

CHAPTER 1—CATCH 22: WHAT TALKING TO THE FBI CAN DO TO YOU

1 For more details on this scenario in the Blagojevich case, see Harvey Silverglate, "Blagojevich's Fatal Unrecorded Conversation," *Forbes*, September 8, 2010.

2 *Id.*

3 Rob Cary, *Not Guilty: The Unlawful Prosecution of U.S. Senator Ted Stevens* (Eagan, Minn.: Thomson Reuters, 2014).

4　Harvey Silverglate, "DOJ's New Recording Policy: The Exceptions Swallow the Rule," *Forbes*, June 2, 2014.

5　Sidney Powell, "New Facts Indicate Mueller Destroyed Evidence, Obstructed Justice," *Daily Caller*, December 16, 2018.

6　For more details on these issues, see Flynn's Brief in Support of His Motion to Compel Production of Brady Material at www.SidneyPowell.com.

7　See Harvey Silverglate, "Constructing Truth: The FBI's (non)recording policy," *Forbes*, July 27, 2011.

8　Senate Judiciary Committee, "Oversight of the Federal Bureau of Investigation," 110th Cong., 1st sess., March 27, 2007, Serial No. J-110-23.

9　*Brogan v. United States*, 322 U.S. 398 (1998).

10　*Commonwealth v. DiGiambattista*, 442 Mass. 423 (2004). In *DiGiambattista*, a suspect made an oral confession in an arson case. Since major aspects of the confession were demonstrably untrue, the Supreme Judicial Court was disturbed over the role the confession might have played in producing the defendant's conviction. This caused the court, exercising its power of "general superintendence" over the operations of the state court system and the system of criminal justice under the Massachusetts Constitution, to announce a rule: In a case where police authorities, for any reason, did not record a confession uttered (or allegedly uttered) by someone in a custodial situation, the trial judge had to instruct the jury, if so requested by a defendant, that "the State's highest court has expressed a preference that such interrogations be recorded whenever practicable." Further, trial judges were directed to caution the jury that, "because of the absence of any recording of the interrogation in the case before them, they should weigh evidence of the defendant's alleged statement with great caution and care." However, this rule, helpful though it is, protects only custodial interviews, not witness interviews, and it does not go far enough when the government holds all the cards and has a greater than 95 percent overall conviction rate.

11　The National Association of Criminal Defense Lawyers (NACDL) has compiled, and regularly updates, a compendium of state policies or court rules requiring the recording of custodial interviews. For the latest version, see "Recording Interrogations," NACDL, https://www.nacdl.org/Landing/RecordingInterrogations, and "Recording Interrogations Reports & Papers," NACDL, https://nacdlwfe1.azurewebsites.net/Content/RecordingInterrogationsReportsPapers.

12　Innocence Project, "False Confessions Happen More Than We Think," https://www.innocenceproject.org/false-confessions-happen-more-than-we-think/.

13　NACDL letter to FBI Director James Comey, December 20, 2013, available at https://nacdlwfe1.azurewebsites.net/Document/LettertoFBIRecordingInterrogations.

14　As a public service initiative at the request of the ACLU of Massachusetts, Harvey Silverglate gave a brief lecture in 2011 for an online video, advising on the dangers of consenting to unrecorded interviews by federal agents. See "Protect Yourself from FBI Manipulation (w/attorney Harvey Silverglate)," ACLU of Massachusetts, published on YouTube, August 13, 2011, http://youtu.be/jgDsbjAYXcQ.

CHAPTER 2—THERE'S NOTHING GRAND ABOUT GRAND JURIES

1   Peter Svab, "Mueller Indicted Ham Sandwich: Lawyer in Russian Troll Farm Case," *Epoch Times*, May 12, 2018.

2   C. Ryan Barber, "DC Judge Tees Up Proof Questions in Mueller's Russian Troll Farm Case," *National Law Journal*, October 15, 2018.

3   As the Supreme Court wrote in *United States v. Bass*, 404 U.S. 336, 348 (1971), "'[A] fair warning should be given to the world in language that the common world will understand, of what the law intends to do if a certain line is passed. To make the warning fair, so far as possible, the line should be clear.' *McBoyle v. United States*, 283 U.S. 25, 27 (1931) (Holmes, J.).....[B]ecause of the seriousness of criminal penalties, and because criminal punishment usually represents the moral condemnation of the community, legislatures, and not courts, should define criminal activity. This policy embodies 'the instinctive distaste against men languishing in prison unless the lawmaker has clearly said they should.' H. Friendly, Mr. Justice Frankfurter and the Reading of Statutes, in Benchmarks 196, 209 (1967).'"

4   For more on the history of the grand jury, going back to English common law, see Greg Glod, "Balancing the Scales of Due Process: The Conservative Case for Grand Jury Reform in Texas," Texas Public Policy Foundation, November 2016, available at http://rightoncrime.com/wp-content/uploads/2016/11/2016-10-PP22-GrandJuryReform-CLG-GregGlod-1-.pdf.

5   Federal Rules of Criminal Procedure, Title III, Rule 6, The Grand Jury, available at https://www.law.cornell.edu/rules/frcrmp.

6   "[Probable cause] 'requires only a probability or substantial chance of criminal activity, not an actual showing of such activity.' Probable cause 'is not a high bar.'" *District of Columbia v. Wesby*, 583 U.S. __ (2018) (at 7) (quoting *Illinois v. Gates*, 462 U.S. 213, 234-244, n. 13 (1983) and *Kaley v. United States*, 571 U.S. __, ___ (2014) (slip op. at 18)).

7   *United States v. Varkonyi*, 611 F.2d 84, 86 (5th Cir.), *cert. denied*, 446 U.S. 945 (1980) (under § 1503, government must prove specific intent to lie).

8   Jed S. Rakoff, "Why Innocent People Plead Guilty," *New York Review of Books*, November 20, 2014.

9   National Association of Criminal Defense Lawyers, *Federal Grand Jury Reform Report and Bill of Rights*, Report of Commission to Reform the Federal Grand Jury, May 18, 2000, available at https://www.nacdl.org/Landing/GrandJury.

10 *Id*. at 9.

11 We considered, and others such as NACDL have recommended, that prosecutors be required to produce to the grand jury any evidence that is exculpatory of the defendant so that the grand jury hears more than the prosecution's side of the case. However, the prosecutor is not going to do nearly as good a job of this as defense counsel would, and could minimize the evidence even as he produced it, so while we encourage this requirement, we favor giving time before the grand jury to counsel for any defendant who wants it.

12 NACDL suggested that the defendant be allowed to testify. (See the "Federal Grand Jury Bill of Rights," No. 4, in *Federal Grand Jury Reform Report and*

Bill of Rights.) We prefer allowing counsel to do it. Usually, the prosecutor rests on the testimony of professional federal agents to prove the charges in an indictment. Allowing defense counsel to make the presentation evens the odds.

13 "A witness before the grand jury who has not received immunity shall have the right to be accompanied by counsel in his or her appearance before the grand jury. Such counsel shall be allowed to be present in the grand jury room only during the questioning of the witness and shall be allowed to advise the witness. Such counsel shall not be permitted to address the grand jurors, stop the proceedings, object to questions, stop the witness from answering a question, nor otherwise take an active part in proceedings before the grand jury. The court shall have the power to remove from the grand jury room, or otherwise sanction counsel for conduct inconsistent with this principle." NACDL, "Federal Grand Jury Bill of Rights," No. 1.

14 In 1935, the Supreme Court pointed out how prosecutors could take advantage of jurors' confidence in their good faith: "The United States Attorney is the representative not of an ordinary party to a controversy, but of a sovereignty whose obligation to govern impartially is as compelling as its obligation to govern at all, and whose interest, therefore, in a criminal prosecution is not that it shall win a case, but that justice shall be done. As such, he is in a peculiar and very definite sense the servant of the law, the two-fold aim of which is that guilt shall not escape or innocence suffer. He may prosecute with earnestness and vigor—indeed, he should do so. But, while he may strike hard blows, he is not at liberty to strike foul ones. It is as much his duty to refrain from improper methods calculated to produce a wrongful conviction as it is to use every legitimate means to bring about a just one.... It is fair to say that the average jury, in a greater or less degree, has confidence that these obligations, which so plainly rest upon the prosecuting attorney, will be faithfully observed. Consequently, improper suggestions, insinuations, and, especially, assertions of personal knowledge are apt to carry much weight against the accused, when they should properly carry none." *Berger v. United States*, 295 U.S. 78, 88 (1935).

CHAPTER 3—ACTS OF GOD

1 *Brady v. Maryland*, 373 U.S. 83, 88 (1963).

2 *Id.*

3 See, for example, *Mooney v. Holohan*, 294 U.S. 103, 112 (1935); *Pyle v. Kansas*, 317 U.S. 213, 215–16. The Fifth Amendment guarantees due process of law in federal criminal cases, while the Fourteenth Amendment extends due process to the states.

4 *Kyles v. Whitley*, 514 U.S. 419, 437 (1995) ("Prosecutors ha[ve] a duty to learn of any favorable evidence known to [] others acting on the government's behalf.").

5 See, for example, *Giglio v. United States*, 405 U.S. 150, 154–55 (1972) (trial prosecutor failed to make sufficient inquiries to discover, and then disclose, promise of leniency made to a prosecution witness by another prosecutor in his office; and prosecutor must disclose any and all "impeachment" material which could impact the credibility of his witnesses); *United States*

v. Agurs, 427 U.S. 97 (1976) (prosecutor is obligated to disclose evidence
that impeaches the credibility of his witness even in the absence of a
specific request by the defense lawyer for such evidence); *United States v.
Bagley*, 473 U.S. 667, 682 (1985) (court clarified the standard by which the
"materiality" of exculpatory material is judged; evidence is "material" when
there is a "reasonable probability" that its disclosure could have affected
guilt or sentence); *Kyles v. Whitley*, 514 U.S. 419, 434 (1995) (prosecutor must
disclose statements in his file or in police files such that withholding the
evidence "undermines confidence" in the trial's outcome—here, the police
had eyewitness statements containing physical descriptions of the attacker
that did not match the defendant); *Banks v. Dretke*, 540 U.S. 668, 693 (2004)
(state failed to disclose that a key witness was a paid government informant
and that another witness's testimony had been coached, and failed to say
something when these witnesses testified falsely on these points).

6 The factual scenario is taken from the post-conviction appellate court
opinion, which in turn took the facts as laid out in a published opinion
in 2006 by the superior court judge who conducted the post-conviction
evidentiary inquiry, spread over a two-year period, pursuant to Baran's
motion for a new trial. *Commonwealth v. Baran*, Docket 07-P-1096, 74 Mass.
App. Ct. 256 (May 15, 2009).

7 "[E]very subject shall have a right to produce all proofs that may be favorable
to him; to meet the witnesses against him face to face, and to be fully heard in
his defense by himself, or his council at his election." Mass. Const. pt. 1. art.
XII.

8 "In all criminal prosecutions, the accused shall enjoy the right ... to have the
assistance of counsel for his defense." U.S. Const. amend. VI.

9 The hearing judge refused to allow Baran's lawyers to call the trial prosecutor,
Daniel Ford, as a witness to testify under oath whether he had turned
over the *unedited* tapes to Baran's trial lawyer or otherwise disclosed to
him the process by which the children had been moved from denying the
abuse had even occurred to accusing Baran of inflicting it. From Baran's
post-conviction counsel's point of view, it was better to take a "belt-and-
suspenders" approach, developing both lines of attack: either Baran's trial
lawyer had the tapes but incompetently failed to use them, or Ford as
prosecutor had engaged in improperly suggestive questioning techniques and
then failed to turn over to Baran's trial lawyer obviously exculpatory material
demonstrating those techniques in action.

For whatever reason, Judge Fecteau took a course that gave Baran the new
trial he demanded, but only on a legal ground that reflected negatively upon
the reputational interest of his by-then deceased trial lawyer, rather than on
a ground that would have cast serious doubt upon the reputation of the trial
prosecutor. In the unlikely event that the grant of a new trial on grounds
of ineffective assistance of counsel were reversed on appeal, Judge Fecteau
could always proceed to decide the second branch of Baran's motion based on
Ford's alleged prosecutorial misconduct. In such a circumstance, Ford would
be called to the witness stand and be given an opportunity to explain, under
oath, his actions or inactions in preparing and trying the case.

The appeals court affirmed the new trial, but it obviously had some insight

into the restrictive way it carried out its obligations: according relief to
Baran but somewhat preserving Ford's reputation. The controlling fact was
that Baran had not received a fair trial, and "preserving public confidence
in the integrity of our system of justice must be our paramount concern
notwithstanding the costs our decision today might occasion." And while
judicial economy was important, the court wrote, "finality should not eclipse
our concern that in our courts justice not miscarry." *Commonwealth v. Baran*,
74 Mass. App. Ct. 256 (May 15, 2009).

10 Judge Ford, via a letter that his attorney John J. Egan wrote to me (Silverglate)
on October 8, 2014, in response to an accusatory op-ed that I wrote about
the case for the *Boston Globe* after Baran's untimely death, denied that he did
not afford Baran's trial lawyer an opportunity to view, pretrial, the unedited
interview tapes. Attorney Egan's letter claims that after the appeals court
published its opinion reversing Baran's conviction and expressing disapproval
of Ford's actions, the Board of Bar Overseers "initiated its own independent
inquiry" and, "after completing its review...took no action." Because BBO
proceedings of that nature are by law closed and secret, I have been unable
to determine precisely what the board did, what it examined, what it knew
and did not know, and what it said. But the bottom line is that somehow the
trial against Bernard Baran proceeded without the jury's ever learning how it
came to be that the child witnesses accused Baran of sexual abuse only after
being worked over by highly improper and suggestive interview and witness
preparation techniques. And if indeed Baran's incompetent trial counsel
did know about the uncut interview tapes and still did not present them to
the jury, one must wonder how the trial judge and even the district attorney
allowed the farce to proceed before the jury.

Indeed, in connection with the BBO inquiry, the former trial judge William
W. Simons, by then long retired, wrote to the board, in a letter effusively
supportive of Ford's character, that Baran's trial lawyer "clearly knew that
there were both edited and unedited versions of the tapes of the interviews
of the children." Yet, wrote Simons, "defense counsel did not insist that they
be played." Simons expressed his belief that defense counsel "had access to all
the tapes in the possession of the district attorney's office, and that if he did
not take advantage of that access, it was by his own choice and not as a result
of any impropriety by Judge [then prosecutor] Ford." In other words, both
Judge Simons and prosecutor Ford knew of the existence of the exculpatory
tapes that decades later would free Baran from a life sentence, but neither one
saw fit to stop the circus in which Baran's defense counsel declined (either
from incompetence or from ignorance of their existence, depending upon
whom one believes) to present them at trial. The rejection of responsibility
for Baran's plight seems to have been a theme in the case until it reached
Judge Fecteau and then the appeals court. The public knows very little of
these shenanigans. See Harvey Silverglate, "Justice system failed Baran: There
should be consequences," *Boston Globe*, October 9, 2014; Editorial, "When
miscarriages of justice occur, prosecutors must answer for actions," *Boston
Globe*, October 19, 2014. The associated correspondence from Judge Ford's
attorney is available on the *Boston Globe* website.

11 North Carolina General Statutes § 15A-903, Disclosure of evidence by the

State—Information subject to disclosure. North Carolina has "a blanket rule of general disclosure." Robert P. Mosteller, "Exculpatory Evidence, Ethics, and the Road to the Disbarment of Mike Nifong: The Critical Importance of Full Open-File Discovery," *George Mason Law Review*, vol. 15, no. 2 (Winter 2008): 257–318, at 260. In 2011, North Carolina even strengthened its open-discovery law, making it a felony for anyone to willfully misrepresent or omit certain information that is required to be disclosed. See John Rubin, "A Rare Opinion on Criminal Discovery in North Carolina," North Carolina Criminal Law, UNC School of Government, May 3, 2016, https://nccriminallaw. sog.unc.edu/rare-opinion-criminal-discovery-north-carolina/. The North Carolina statute would be an excellent model for adoption by Congress or the federal courts, and is included in the Appendices.

12 Texas Code of Criminal Procedure, Article 39.14, Discovery. Referred to as the "Michael Morton Act," the statute requires the prosecutor to provide the defense with all nonprivileged material in possession of any state actor "as soon as practicable" after request, and the prosecution must "disclose to the defendant any exculpatory, impeachment, or mitigating document, item, or information in the possession, custody, or control of the State that tends to negate the guilt of the defendant or would tend to reduce the punishment for the offense charged." https://www.versustexas.com/cpp-39-14/.

13 Florida Criminal Code, Rule 3.220, Discovery, https:// floridacriminalprocedure.com/3-220-discovery/.

14 Florida's reciprocal discovery rules provide, for example, that a defendant may secure an opportunity to take "discovery depositions" of witnesses, but the defense understands that the prosecutor has a reciprocal ability to learn the identity of, and depose, defense witnesses. This system is a radical departure from the traditional "adversary system" in which prosecutors for the most part keep their strategies secret (with the exception of the obligation to disclose exculpatory material), and defendants enjoy even broader ability to play their cards close to the vest (with no obligation for the most part to disclose defense witnesses, nor even to disclose whether the defendant will testify in his own behalf, much less what the defendant would say).

Interestingly, the Florida reciprocal criminal discovery system has a provision under which one side may "move for an order denying or regulating disclosure of sensitive matters," and such issues may be heard and decided *in camera* (that is, in the judge's chambers rather than in the open courtroom), presumably, in certain circumstances, with only one side present. Thus, a party may explain to the judge, without the other side's learning, the reasons why a certain request is being made. And the confidentiality of government informants remains protected, at least unless and until a witness is called to testify at the trial, by a provision in the rule that the government disclose any deals made with such a witness, without revealing the identity of the informant except in very limited and narrow circumstances.

15 Hon. Alex Kozinski, Preface, "Criminal Law 2.0," *Georgetown Law Journal Annual Review of Criminal Procedure*, vol. 44 (2015).

16 *Id.* at viii, citing *United States v. Olsen*, 737 F.3d 625, 626 (9th Cir. 2013) (Kozinski, J., dissenting from denial of rehearing *en banc*).

17 *Frost v. Gilbert*, 818 F.3d 469 (9th Cir. 2016) (*en banc*). This was a federal

18 *habeas corpus* attack on a criminal conviction in a state court in the state of Washington.

18 The *Frost* case was admittedly a difficult one since the defendant's guilt was quite clear, unlike the cases discussed in Chapter 9 concerning the degradation of federal *habeas corpus* protections. But Judge Kozinski took advantage of his platform in that case to ask why no disciplinary inquiry was undertaken concerning the apparent prosecutorial misconduct.

19 Kozinski's opinion was amended later that year, when the Washington State Bar Association Office of Disciplinary Counsel dismissed a grievance against the prosecutor Kozinski excoriated for his *Brady* violations. The amended opinion is *Frost v. Gilbert* 835 F.3d 883 (9th Cir. 2016).

20 Jan Ransom and Ashley Southall, "Prosecutors Sometimes Behave Badly. Now They May Be Held to Account," *New York Times*, April 5, 2019. John Hollway proposed such a commission and a number of other basic reforms aimed at increasing prosecutorial accountability in "Reining in Prosecutorial Misconduct," *Wall Street Journal*, July 4, 2016.

21 See, for example, the Innocence Project, "Prosecutorial Oversight: A National Dialogue in the Wake of *Connick v. Thompson*," March 2016, dealing with a wide array of prosecutorial misconduct resulting in wrongful convictions.

22 The details of the Stevens case are readily available from press reports; a book written after the case ended by one of Stevens's lawyers, Rob Cary, *Not Guilty: The Unlawful Prosecution of U.S. Senator Ted Stevens* (Eagan, Minn.: Thomson Reuters, 2014); Powell, *Licensed to Lie*; and the so-called Schuelke Report.

23 Powell, *Licensed to Lie*, Epilogue.

CHAPTER 4—WHAT DOES THE LAW REQUIRE OF US?

1 U.S.C. § 596.

2 *United States v. Rafiekian*, No. 1:18-cr-457-AJT-1 (E.D. Va. Sept. 24, 2019).

3 The jury convicted Rafiekian even though there was not even enough evidence to support the admission of co-conspirators' statements as an exception to the rule against hearsay, and the government had no evidence to meet its own definition of "materiality" or articulate how the conduct was criminal. Notably, Judge Anthony Trenga (Eastern District of Virginia), in a thorough and brilliant decision, granted a judgment of acquittal to defendant Rafiekian. *United States v. Rafiekian*, No. 1:18-cr-457-AJT-1 (E.D. Va. Sept. 24, 2019), https://scholar.google.com/scholar_case?case=8948258015535804129&q=United+States+v.+Rafiekian&hl=en&as_sdt=6,44.

4 *United States v. Dotterweich*, 320 U.S. 277 (1943).

5 *Id.* at 285.

6 *Morissette v. United States*, 342 U.S. 246 (1952).

7 18 U.S.C. § 922(g).

8 *Rehaif v. United States*, 588 U.S. ____ (2019).

9 *Elonis v. United States*, 135 S. Ct. 2001 (2015).

10 *Id.* at 2012.

11 Senate Judiciary Committee, "Hatch, Grassley Introduce Bill to Strengthen and Clarify Intent Requirements in Federal Criminal Law," Press Release, June

22, 2018, https://www.judiciary.senate.gov/press/rep/releases/hatch-grassley-introduce-bill-to-strengthen-and-clarify-intent-requirements-in-federal-criminal-law.

12 Brian W. Walsh and Tiffany M. Joslyn, "Without Intent: How Congress Is Eroding the Criminal Intent Requirement in Federal Law," Heritage Foundation and NACDL, 2010, at 6–7.

13 *Id.* at 7.

14 18 U.S.C. § 596.

15 *Morissette*, 342 U.S. at 251–52.

16 *Id.* at 274–76.

17 Walsh and Joslyn, "Without Intent," xi–xiii.

18 *Id.* at 32.

19 See *New State Ice Co. v. Liebmann*, 285 U.S. 262, 311 (1932) (Brandeis, J., dissenting).

20 Lee Dryden, "Default *Mens Rea* Standard Signed into Law," *Detroit Legal News*, January 13, 2016, http://legalnews.com/detroit/1418937.

21 Jason Hayes, "A State-Made Wetland Problem," *Detroit News*, July 12, 2017.

22 *People v. Taylor*, No. 295275, 2012 WL 1890190, at *5 (Mich. Ct. App. May 22, 2012) (holding that defense's failure to object at trial to jury instructions on strict liability offense waived appeal of the issue).

23 *People v. Taylor*, 844 N.W.2d 707, 710 (Mich. 2014) (Markman, J., concurring).

24 Dryden, "Default *Mens Rea* Standard Signed into Law."

25 See John G. Malcolm, "Morally Innocent, Legally Guilty: The Case for Mens Rea Reform," *Federalist Society Review*, vol. 18 (2017): 40–47, at 44.

26 Chuck Grassley and Orrin Hatch, "*Mens Rea* Reform and the Criminal Justice Reform Constellation," *Washington Examiner*, July 19, 2018.

27 John-Michael Seibler and John Malcolm, "Criminal Justice Reform a Big Part of Orrin Hatch's Legacy," Heritage Foundation, June 25, 2018.

28 Grassley and Hatch, "*Mens Rea* Reform and the Criminal Justice Reform Constellation."

29 Matt Ford, "The Criminal-Justice Reform Bill Is Both Historic and Disappointing," *New Republic*, December 12, 2018.

30 See Rachel Bade, Daniel Lippmann, and Sarah Wheaton, "Senate strikes compromise on criminal justice reform," *Politico*, September 30, 2015.

31 Matt Ford, "Could a Controversial Bill Sink Criminal-Justice Reform in Congress?" *Atlantic*, October 26, 2017.

32 *Id.*

33 Greg Dotson and Alison Cassady, "Three Ways Congressional *Mens Rea* Proposals Could Allow White Collar Criminals to Escape Prosecution," Center for American Progress, March 11, 2016.

34 Ira M. Feinberg, Chair of New York City Bar, letter to Sens. Grassley et al., August 16, 2016, https://s3.amazonaws.com/documents.nycbar.org/files/20073138-MensReaReformCrimCodeImprovement_FedCourt_FINAL_8.16.16.pdf.

35 Alex Sarch, "How to solve the biggest issue holding up criminal justice reform," *Politico: The Agenda*, May 16, 2016; Gideon Yaffe, Opinion, "A Republican Crime Proposal That Democrats Should Back," *New York Times*, February 12, 2016.

36 Benjamin Levin, "*Mens Rea* Reform and Its Discontents," *Journal of Criminal Law and Criminology*, vol. 109, no. 3 (Summer 2019): 491–558, at 497.

37 *Id.* at 522.

38 *Id.* at 535. A district judge expressed this concept in a sentencing in one of Sidney Powell's recent cases. She had argued in general for criminal justice reform and against over-incarceration. The judge's response was to note her client's life of white privilege and say that he should go to prison. But the remedy for these wrongs is not to imprison businessmen more; it is to imprison others less, except the dangerous or those likely to flee.

39 Bureau of Justice Statistics, "Prison and Jail Incarceration Rates Decreased by More Than 10% from 2007 to 2017," Press Release, April 25, 2019, https://www.bjs.gov/content/pub/press/p17ji17pr.cfm.

40 See generally Wendy W. Williams, "Ruth Bader Ginsburg's Equal Protection Clause: 1979–80," *Columbia Journal of Gender and Law*, vol. 25 (2103): 41–49 (discussing various contemporaneous criticisms of Ginsburg's strategy).

41 *Ratzlaf v. United States*, 510 U.S. 135 (1994).

42 *Id.* at 148.

43 See, e.g., Mireille Hildebrandt, "Justice and Police: Regulatory Offenses and the Criminal Law," *New Criminal Law Review*, vol. 12, no. 1 (Winter 2009): 43–68, at 68. "If the punishment of regulatory offenses is to achieve its target (of compliance) the punishment must entail a process of communication that includes the possibility of the accused contesting the wrongfulness of her action or the lawfulness of the violated rule."

44 *United States v. Bass*, 404 U.S. 336, 347-49 (1971) (First, as we have recently reaffirmed, "ambiguity concerning the ambit of criminal statutes should be resolved in favor of lenity.") (quoting *Rewis v. United States*, 401 U. S. 808, 812 (1971)). *See also Ladner v. United States*, 358 U. S. 169, 177 (1958); *Bell v. United States*, 349 U.S. 81 (1955); *United States v. Five Gambling Devices*, 346 U.S. 441 (1953) (plurality opinion for affirmance). In various ways over the years, we have stated that "when choice has to be made between two readings of what conduct Congress has made a crime, it is appropriate, before we choose the harsher alternative, to require that Congress should have spoken in language that is clear and definite." *United States v. Universal C. I. T. Credit Corp.*, 344 U.S. 218, 221-22 (1952). This principle is founded on two policies that have long been part of our tradition. First, "a fair warning should be given to the world in language that the common world will understand, of what the law intends to do if a certain line is passed. To make the warning fair, so far as possible the line should be clear." *McBoyle v. United States*, 283 U. S. 25, 27 (1931) (Holmes, J.); *see also United States v. Cardiff*, 344 U.S. 174 (1952). Second, because of the seriousness of criminal penalties, and because criminal punishment usually represents the moral condemnation of the community, legislatures and not courts should define criminal activity. This policy embodies "the instinctive distaste against men languishing in prison unless the lawmaker has clearly said they should." H. Friendly, Mr. Justice Frankfurter and the Reading of Statutes, in Benchmarks 196, 209 (1967). Thus, where there is ambiguity in a criminal statute, doubts are resolved in favor of the defendant. Here, we conclude that Congress has not "plainly and unmistakably," *United States v. Gradwell*, 243 U.S. 476, 485 (1917), made

it a federal crime for a convicted felon simply to possess a gun absent some demonstrated nexus with interstate commerce.

There is a second principle supporting today's result: unless Congress conveys its purpose clearly, it will not be deemed to have significantly changed the federal-state balance. Congress has traditionally been reluctant to define as a federal crime conduct readily denounced as criminal by the States. This congressional policy is rooted in the same concepts of American federalism that have provided the basis for judge-made doctrines. *See, e.g., Younger* v. *Harris,* 401 U.S. 37 (1971). As this Court emphasized only last Term in *Rewis* v. *United States, supra,* we will not be quick to assume that Congress has meant to effect a significant change in the sensitive relation between federal and state criminal jurisdiction.)

CHAPTER 5—PLEA BARGAINING: DANCING WITH THE DEVIL

1 U.S. Sentencing Commission, *Sourcebook of Federal Sentencing Statistics,* Fiscal Year 2017, at 25, available at https://www.ussc.gov/research/sourcebook-2017.

2 See the Innocence Project, "When the Innocent Plead Guilty," for more information on state convictions based on false confessions compelled by the "system," at https://www.innocenceproject.org/when-the-innocent-plead-guilty/.

3 Jed S. Rakoff, "Why Innocent People Plead Guilty," *New York Review of Books,* November 20, 2014.

4 We have many issues with the federal sentencing guidelines, which are mechanistic and all but controlling, despite the Supreme Court's declaring them "guidelines" only in *United States v. Booker,* 543 U.S. 220 (2005). At the same time, prosecutors can manipulate them by the kind of offenses they charge, the number of offenses, and in financial cases the amount of money they allege to be involved.

We encourage abolition of the U.S. Sentencing Commission and abolition of mandatory minimum sentences in all but the most heinous offenses. Federal judges should have far more discretion to fashion alternatives to incarceration—especially for nonviolent offenses. Respectable studies show that six years in prison is a very long time, and it becomes extremely difficult for someone to reintegrate into society after being incarcerated longer than that.

5 The Office of Special Counsel was forced to admit as much at what was supposed to be Flynn's sentencing hearing on December 18, 2018. Transcript of Sentencing Proceedings in *United States v. Flynn,* No. 17-cr-232-EGS, 34-36 (D.D.C. Dec. 18, 2018), https://www.justsecurity.org/wp-content/uploads/2018/12/121818am-USA-v-Michael-Flynn-Sentencing.pdf.

6 See Lee Smith, *The Plot to Destroy the President: The True Story of How Congressman Devin Nunes Uncovered the Biggest Political Scandal in U.S. History* (New York: Center Street, Hachette Book Group, 2019).

7 Kristen Hays, "Judge allows withdrawal of guilty plea in Enron case," *Houston Chronicle,* April 3, 2007.

8 "Charge dropped against accountant David Duncan," *Houston Chronicle,* December 15, 2005. As it turned out, the conviction of Arthur Andersen

was unanimously reversed by the Supreme Court. Weissmann and Leslie Caldwell—both in the Bush Department of Justice at the time—destroyed the company without any legal basis for doing so. *Arthur Andersen LLP v. United States*, No. 04–368 (May 31, 2005), https://www.supremecourt.gov/opinions/04pdf/04-368.pdf.

9   Comey uttered the remarks in an interview with Nicolle Wallace, NBC News political analyst. See "James Comey in Conversation with Nicolle Wallace," 92nd Street Y, published on YouTube, December 10, 2018, https://www.youtube.com/watch?v=9xqGu66D6VU. He further elaborated on his comments in an interview with the House Judiciary Committee. See: Committee on the Judiciary and Committee on Oversight and Government Reform, "Interview: James Comey," U.S. House of Representatives, December 17, 2018, at 20, https://www.scribd.com/document/395969146/Comey-Interview-Dec-17#from_embed.

10   Plea Agreement in *United States v. Cohen*, No. 18-cr-850-WHP (Nov. 29, 2018).

11   While this book does not purport to address prison reform, we vehemently urge the Department of Justice to bar the use of solitary confinement for any purpose other than to control those prisoners who cannot be controlled by any other means. Both the ACLU and the UN have declared solitary confinement to be torture. The Bureau of Prisons is rife with corruption and in dire need of major reform. See Bernard Kerik, *From Jailer to Jailed: My Journey from Correction and Police Commissioner to Inmate #84888-054* (New York: Threshold Editions, 2015).

12   The National Registry of Exonerations, which includes both federal and state prisoners, can be found at https://www.law.umich.edu/special/exoneration/Pages/about.aspx.

13   U.S. Const. amend. VI.

14   U.S.S.G. § 3C1.1.

15   U.S.S.G. § 3E1.1. This provision has long been automatically denied to those who go to trial. It was amended in 2018 to make it a little easier for a defendant who goes to trial to seek a decrease in his offense level, but this change does not seem to have had any real-world effect. See Grand Jury Target, "New Sentencing Guidelines Have Two Good Provisions for White Collar Criminal Defendants (and Lawyers)," November 8, 2018, https://grandjurytarget.com/2018/11/08/new-proposed-sentencing-guidelines-have-some-good-provisions-for-white-collar-criminal-defendants-and-lawyers/.

CHAPTER 6—AN OFFER HE CAN'T REFUSE

1   Maria Cramer and Travis Anderson, "Witnesses raised Bulger jurors' ire, suspicions," *Boston Globe*, August 13, 2013.

2   Denise Lavoie, "John Martorano, Ex–Winter Hill Gangster, Continues Testimony Against Whitey Bulger," *Huffington Post*, June 19, 2013.

3   Shelley Murphy and Milton J. Valencia, "Confessed murderer ties Bulger to 6 killings," *Boston Globe*, June 17, 2013.

4   Plea Agreement in *United States v. Flemmi*, No. 99-cr-10371-RGS (D. Mass. Oct. 2, 2003), http://www.ipsn.org/characters/flemmi/flemmi_agreement.pdf.

5   *Id.*

6 The death penalty is available in a certain category of serious federal crimes, even when a federal trial is conducted in a federal court located in a state that has abolished the death penalty. For example, the Boston Marathon bomber, Dzhokhar Tsarnaev, was convicted and sentenced to death in Boston's federal court in 2015 under a federal terrorism statute allowing for capital punishment. Had he been tried in state court for murder under Massachusetts law, the maximum penalty would have been life without parole. Federal authorities can ratchet up the available penalties in a case where there is both state and federal (so-called "concurrent") jurisdiction. This poses challenges to public perceptions of justice when state procedures are perceived—often rightly so—as fairer than the cognate federal practices.

7 *United States v. Dennis*, 183 F.2d 201 (2nd Cir. 1950), aff'd. 341 U.S. 494 (1951). A conspiracy is generally defined as an agreement by two or more individuals to commit a criminal act. In some state jurisdictions, a conspiracy may be prosecuted only after the conspirators have taken at least one "overt act" to further the agreement. Conspiracy is widely viewed as the most inchoate of all crimes in state and federal criminal codes, since it consists more of an agreement than of an attempted or accomplished crime. Some courts—at the urging of the government—have even defined it as an "understanding," even though an understanding can be entirely unilateral. Conspiracies are dangerously easy to charge and to prove. It is the rare judge, such as Anthony Trenga, in *United States v. Rafiekian* in the Eastern District of Virginia, who will hold that the government has failed to prove a criminal conspiracy. *United States v. Rafiekian*, No. 1:18-cr-457-AJT-1, 2019 WL 4647254 (E.D. Va. Sept. 24, 2019). *Licensed to Lie* reveals how very easy it is for the government to turn an innocent commercial transaction into a "criminal conspiracy" long enough to fool a jury and often an appellate court.

8 *United States v. Dennis*, 183 F.2d 201 (2nd Cir. 1950), aff'd. 341 U.S. 494 (1951).

9 18 U.S.C. § 371.

10 18 U.S.C. § 2.

11 18 U.S.C. §§ 1341, 1343, and 1346.

12 The nonprofit Families Against Mandatory Minimums (FAMM) has compiled a list of federal mandatory minimums, available at https://famm.org/wp-content/uploads/Chart-All-Fed-MMs.pdf.

13 Alexandra Natapoff, *Snitching: Criminal Informants and the Erosion of American Justice* (New York: New York University Press, 2009).

14 Senator Edward "Ted" Kennedy (D. Mass.), for example, praised Stephen Breyer at his Supreme Court confirmation hearings: "In his decisions [Justice Breyer] has construed the Constitution to defend the basic rights of all Americans.... As one of the first members of the sentencing commission, he is widely credited with developing the guidelines to reduce the disparities in sentences given to defendants committing similar crimes." See the Breyer Confirmation Hearing Day 1 Part 1, C-SPAN, July 12, 1994, at 29:00, http://www.c-span.org/video/?58601-1/breyer-confirmation-hearing-day-1-part-1.

15 18 U.S.C. § 3553(e) provides that "Upon motion of the Government, the court shall have the authority to impose a sentence below a level established by statute as a minimum sentence so as to reflect a defendant's substantial assistance in the investigation or prosecution of another person who has committed an offense."

16 U.S.S.G. § 5K1.1 provides that "Upon motion of the government stating that the defendant has provided substantial assistance in the investigation or prosecution of another person who has committed an offense, the court may depart from the Guidelines." In addition, the Federal Rules of Criminal Procedure, Rule 35, permits courts (if petitioned by the government) to reduce a cooperating defendant's sentence years after it has been imposed. There thus remains a strong incentive for convicted prisoners to testify for the government after they have tasted the full displeasure of residing in a federal detention facility.

17 Carl Takei, "Terrorizing Justice: An Argument That Plea Bargains Struck Under the Threat of 'Enemy Combatant' Detention Violate the Right to Due Process," *Boston College Law Review*, vol. 47, no. 3 (May 2006): 581–626. Mr. Takei was a research assistant for Harvey Silverglate from 2002 until 2004.

18 For a full explanation of this process and the abuses it creates, please read Judith Miller, *The Story: A Reporter's Journey* (New York: Simon & Schuster, 2015). See Clarice Feldman, "New revelation helps exonerate Scooter Libby," *American Thinker*, April 7, 2015.

19 This is not to say, of course, that the problem of rewarded witnesses—with the full extent of the rewards rarely laid out for the jurors to learn—is not well recognized by criminal justice professionals and other participants in the system. See, for example, Stephen S. Trott, "The Use of Criminal as Witness: A Special Problem," Lecture Supplement, ACLU, October 2007, https://www.aclu.org/files/pdfs/drugpolicy/informant_trott_outline.pdf; Jim Dwyer, Peter Neufeld, and Barry Scheck, *Actual Innocence: Five Days to Execution and Other Dispatches from the Wrongly Convicted* (New York: Doubleday, 2000), 126–57.

20 See *Ostrer vs. Aronwald*, 434 F.Supp. 379 (S.D.N.Y. 1977), *affirmed* 567 F.2d 551 (2nd Cir., 1977).

21 *United States v. Singleton* is discussed in some detail in Silverglate, *Three Felonies a Day*, xlviii–xlviii.

22 *United States v. Singleton*, 165 F.3d 1297 (10th Cir. 1999, *en banc*).

23 *United States v. Waterman*, 732 F.2d 1527 (8th Cir. 1984).

24 *United States v. Dailey*, 589 F.Supp. 561 (D. Mass 1984); *United States v. Dailey*, 759 F.2d 192 (1st Cir. 1985).

25 18 U.S.C. § 401.

CHAPTER 7—PROSECUTORIAL MISCONDUCT

1 Justice Brandeis Law Project, "Causes of Wrongful Convictions: Misconduct by Prosecutors or Law Enforcement," The Schuster Institute for Investigative Journalism, Brandeis University, https://www.brandeis.edu/investigate/innocence-project/police-misconduct.html.

2 Project on Government Oversight, "Hundreds of Justice Department Attorneys Violated Professional Rules, Laws, or Ethical Standards," March 12, 2014, http://pogoarchives.org/m/ga/opr-report-20140312.pdf.

3 Robert H. Jackson, "The Federal Prosecutor," in *Journal of Criminal Law & Criminology*, vol. 31, no. 1 (May/June 1940): 3–6. Jackson's speech should be the mantra of the Department of Justice, and required reading for all attorneys general and United States attorneys and their assistants.

4   "[I]t is appropriate to judge selective prosecution claims according to ordinary equal protection standards." *United States v. Wayte*, 470 U.S. 598, 608 (1985). See *Boling v. Sharpe*, 340 U.S. 497, 500 (1954). To justify selective enforcement of the law, and assuming no suspect category is involved, the government must have a rational basis for its selection. See *Dixon*, 394 F.2d at 968 ("[T]he Government employs an impermissible classification when it punishes those who complain against [prosecutorial] misconduct and excuses those who do not."). And, "[a] showing of discriminatory intent is not necessary when the equal protection claim is based on an overtly discriminatory classification." *Wayte*, 470 U.S. at 608 n.10. *United States v. Bass*, 536 U.S. 862, 863-64 (2002) (*per curiam*) ("[A] defendant who seeks discovery on a claim of selective prosecution must show some evidence of both discriminatory effect and discriminatory intent.").

5   See *Yates v. United States*, 135 S. Ct. 1074 (2015), https://www.supremecourt. gov/opinions/14pdf/13-7451_m640.pdf.

6   Buzz Lightyear in *Toy Story* (Pixar, 1995).

7   Editorial, "Arthur Andersen's 'Victory,'" *Wall Street Journal*, June 1, 2005.

8   *Arthur Andersen LLP v. United States*, 544 U.S. 696 (2005), https://www. supremecourt.gov/opinions/04pdf/04-368.pdf.

9   Sidney Powell, "How Did the Wife of a Mueller Protégé End Up Hearing Mueller's Case?" *Daily Caller*, January 10, 2019.

10   See *United States v. Bass*, 404 U.S. 336, 348 (1971) ("a fair warning should be given to the world in language that the common world will understand, of what the law intends to do if a certain line is passed.").

11   Andrew Weissmann and the prosecutors in the Enron case first charged Andrew Fastow, Enron's chief financial officer and the architect of Enron's frauds, in a hefty criminal complaint. When Fastow still did not break and cooperate, they added thirty-one more counts for a total of seventy-eight and indicted his wife on six counts. Lloyd Vries, "New Slew of Enron Indictments," CBS News, November 2, 2002; "Ex-Enron CFO Fastow indicted on 78 counts," *Houston Chronicle*, October 31, 2002.

     Fastow was still holding out on "cooperating" with Weissmann and soon found himself indicted on 109 counts and his wife going to prison. *United States v. Fastow*, 269 F. Supp. 2d 905 (S.D. Tex. 2003). By "cooperating" to Weissmann's satisfaction, Fastow saw his life sentence reduced to six years—even though his plea agreement had said he would receive ten years. Federal Bureau of Investigation, "Former Enron Chief Financial Officer Andrew Fastow Pleads Guilty to Conspiracy to Commit Securities and Wire Fraud, Agrees to Cooperate with Enron Investigation," Press Release, January 14, 2004, https://archives.fbi.gov/archives/news/pressrel/press-releases/former-enron-chief-financial-officer-andrew-fastow-pleads-guilty-to-conspiracy-to-commit-securities-and-wire-fraud; Department of Justice, "Former Enron Chief Financial Officer Andrew Fastow Sentenced to Six Years in Prison for Conspiracy to Commit Securities and Wire Fraud," September 26, 2006, https://www.justice.gov/criminal-vns/case/fastowa; and Powell, *Licensed to Lie*, 99, 101, 410.

12   The full indictment of Skilling and Lay (U.S. District Court, Southern

District of Texas) is available here: http://www.ussguide.com/members/
BulletinBoard/Blakely/KennethLayIndictment.pdf.

13 *Skilling v. United States*, 554 F.3d 529 (5th Cir. 2009), Petition for Writ of
Certiorari.

14 This targeting began before Mueller was appointed special counsel and
Weissmann joined as his lieutenant. Weissmann is supposedly under
investigation for his coordination with Associated Press reporters as he
targeted Manafort while Weissmann was head of the fraud section at the
Department of Justice. See Chuck Ross, "Mueller's 'Pit Bull' Arranged
Meeting with Reporters to Discuss Manafort Investigation," *Daily Caller*, July
8, 2018; Thomas Lifson, "Shocker: AP and FBI seemingly in collaboration in
Manafort investigation," *American Thinker*, July 8, 2018; Rachel Weiner, "Paul
Manafort wants investigation into a member of Mueller's team," *Washington
Post*, May 21, 2018.

15 Brooke Singman, "Manafort ordered to jail, bail revoked on witness
tampering charge," Fox News, June 15, 2018.

16 The ACLU and the United Nations have declared solitary confinement a form
of torture. For someone like Paul Manafort, who had no previous encounter
with the prison system, it is beyond the pale. See Sidney Powell, "Manafort's
Torture Shows Character of Mueller's Goon Squad," *Daily Caller*, January 9,
2019; Bernard Kerik, *From Jailer to Jailed: My Journey from Correction and
Police Commissioner to Inmate #84888-054* (New York: Threshold Editions,
2015).

17 Mark Berman, "FBI director blasts 'mind-boggling' shutdown impact in
message to unpaid employees," *Washington Post*, January 25, 2019.

18 Joe Dwinell, "FBI's Roger Stone raid sends chilling message," *Boston Herald*,
January 26, 2019.

19 The pleadings in *United States v. Flynn* that document this issue are available
at www.SidneyPowell.com.

20 The Foreign Agents Registration Act, signed into law after World War II, has
rarely been enforced. See Ken Silverstein, "I've Covered Foreign Lobbying for
20 Years and I'm Amazed Manafort Got Busted," *Politico*, October 30, 2017.

21 Victor Morton, "Mueller reportedly grants Tony Podesta immunity to testify
against Paul Manafort," *Washington Times*, July 19, 2018; Julia Ainsley, Tom
Winter, and Carol E. Lee, "Sources: Podesta Group, Mercury Are Companies
'A' and 'B' in Indictment," NBC News, October 30, 2017; John Sexton,
"Podesta Group Employees Told the Company Is Shutting Down," *Hot Air*,
November 11, 2017.

22 "Congressman Matt Gaetz Unveils the Justice For All Resolution," Office of
Matt Gaetz, U.S. House of Representatives, Press Release, February 4, 2019,
https://gaetz.house.gov/media/press-releases/congressman-matt-gaetz-
unveils-justice-all-resolution.

23 *Yick Wo v. Hopkins*, 118 U.S. 356, 373-74 (1886). See also, *United States
v. Wayte*, 470 U.S. 598, 6088 (1985) ("It is appropriate to judge selective
prosecution claims according to ordinary equal protection standards.");
United States v. Lawrence, 179 F.3d 343, 349-50 (5th Cir. 1999), *cert. denied*,
528 U.S. 1096 (2000) (government must have a reasonable and proper basis
upon which to apply disparate treatment to similarly situated individuals).

24 See *Bordenkircher v. Hayes*, 434 U.S. 357, 364 (1978) ("[S]o long as the

prosecutor has probable cause to believe that the accused committed an offense defined by statute, the decision whether or not to prosecute, and what charge to file or bring before the grand jury, generally rests entirely in his discretion."). *Accord Wayte*, 470 U.S. at 607.

25 See *United States v. Goodwin*, 457 U.S. 368, 384 (1982) (recognizing possibility that defendant may show objectively "that the prosecutor's charging decision was motivated by a desire to punish him for doing something that the law plainly allowed him to do," and was therefore violative of the Equal Protection Clause); *id.* at 380 n.11 (1982) ("A charging decision does not levy an improper 'penalty' unless it results solely from the defendant's exercise of a protected legal right, rather than the prosecutor's normal assessment of the societal interest in prosecution."); *United States v. Steele*, 461 F.2d 1148, 1152 (9th Cir. 1972).

26 Powell, *Licensed to Lie*, 384.

27 *United States v. Brown*, 459 F.3d 509, 517 (5th Cir. 2006).

28 Report of the Inspector General of the Department of Justice, Findings of Misconduct by a Then Deputy Assistant Attorney General for Misuse of DOJ-Issued Computers and for False Statements, August 19, 2019, https://oig.justice.gov/reports/2019/f190829.pdf.

CHAPTER 8—WHERE HAVE ALL THE JUDGES GONE?

1 James M. Burnham, "Why Don't Courts Dismiss Indictments? A Simple Suggestion for Making Federal Criminal Law a Little Less Lawless," *Green Bag*, vol. 18, no. 4 (Summer 2015): 347–62.

2 Alan M. Gershowitz, "Prosecutorial Shaming: Naming Attorneys to Reduce Prosecutorial Misconduct," *UC Davis Law Review*, vol. 42, no. 4 (April 2009): 1059–1105.

3 Burnham, "Why Don't Courts Dismiss Indictments?" at 348.

4 *McNabb* v. *United States*, 318 U. S. 332 (1943).

5 Nathan E. Ross, "Nearly Forgotten Supervisory Power: The Wrench to Retaining the Miranda Warnings," *Missouri Law Review*, vol. 66, no. 4 (Fall 2001): 849–80.

6 Jim Drinkhall, "CIA Helped Quash Major, Star-Studded Tax Evasion Case," *Washington Post*, April 24, 1980 (originally printed in the *Wall Street Journal*).

7 *United States v. Payner*, 447 U.S. 727 (1980).

8 In the wake of the government's destruction of Arthur Andersen, the KPMG accounting firm, when threatened with an indictment, caved in and entered into a deferred prosecution agreement so onerous, and so manipulative, that the district judge intervened to negate one of its key provisions: that KPMG would cancel its otherwise enforceable obligation to pay for legal counsel for its indicted individual employees. The DPA also required that KPMG provide testimony that certain tax shelters, which it had devised and had consistently defended up until that point, were in fact illegal. In short, the Department of Justice was seeking, via the DPA, to disable the defense by depriving them of money for legal fees, while coercing a cooperating company to provide testimony favorable to the government's version of the facts, even if not true. See Silverglate, *Three Felonies a Day*, 146–52.

9 *United States v. HSBC Bank USA*, 12-cr-763 (EDNY 2013), Memorandum and Order (July 1, 2013).

10 *United States v. Fokker Services B.V.*, 79 F.Supp.3d 160 (D.D.C. 2015), *reversed*, 818 F.3d 733 (D.C. Cir. 2016).

11 *Id.* at 166.

12 *United States v. Fokker Services B.V.*, 818 F.3d 733 (D.C. Cir. 2016).

13 *Id.* at 738.

14 50 U.S.C. ch. 36 § 1801 et seq.

15 Rosemary M. Collyer, Memorandum Opinion and Order, FISA Ct. (Apr. 26, 2017), https://www.dni.gov/files/documents/icotr/51117/2016_Cert_FISC_Memo_Opin_Order_Apr_2017.pdf; James E. Boasberg, Memorandum Opinion and Order, FISA Ct. (Oct. 18, 2018), https://www.intelligence.gov/assets/documents/702%20Documents/declassified/2018_Cert_FISC_Opin_18Oct18.pdf.

16 Amy Coney Barrett, "The Supervisory Power of the Supreme Court," *Columbia Law Review*, vol. 106, no. 2 (March 2006): 324–87, especially at 328, 363.

CHAPTER 9—ONCE IS NOT ENOUGH

1 Joe McGinniss, *Fatal Vision* (New York: G. P. Putnam's Sons, 1983). See also the counternarrative book, which in my opinion is the more factual and reliable account: Jerry Allen Potter and Fred Bost, *Fatal Justice* (New York: W. W. Norton & Co., 1995).

2 *Fatal Vision*, 1984 made-for-tv movie, starring Karl Malden and Eva Marie Saint.

3 U.S. Const. art. I, § 9, cl. 2.

4 "The Laws of the United States: Acts of the First Congress of the United States," Session 1 (1798), chap. 20, sec. 14, in *A Century of Lawmaking for a New Nation: U.S. Congressional Documents and Debates, 1774–1875*, Library of Congress, pp. 81–82, http://memory.loc.gov/cgi-bin/ampage?collId=llsl&fileName=001/llsl001.db&recNum=204. The current iteration of the All Writs Act is codified as 28 U.S.C. § 1651.

5 See Dimitri D. Portnoi, "Resorting to Extraordinary Writs: How the All Writs Act Rises to Fill the Gaps in the Rights of Enemy Combatants," *New York University Law Review*, vol. 81, no. 1 (2008): 293–332. As Portnoi notes, judicial power under the All Writs Act is not unlimited. The act was intended only as a "gap-filler"; the courts could act only as de facto legislators on issues unaddressed by Congress.

6 *McCleskey v. Zant*, 499 U.S. 467 (1991).

7 For a complete overview of the history of, and the differences between, § 2255 and *habeas corpus* petitions, see Harvard Law Review Association, "Suspended Justice: The Case Against 28 U.S.C. § 2255's Statute of Limitations," Notes, *Harvard Law Review*, vol. 129, no. 4 (February 2016). Federal prisoners technically still have access to *habeas corpus* relief proper under 28 U.S.C. § 2241, but in practice § 2255 motions are the only avenue for collateral attacks on convictions in federal court.

8 More details on this aspect of the MacDonald case are available in Harvey Silverglate's article, "Reflections on the Jeffrey MacDonald Case," *The Champion* magazine, National Association of Criminal Defense Lawyers, May 2013, http://www.nacdl.org/Champion.aspx?id=28481. Further

invaluable insight into the case can be gained from the book by the
documentarian Errol Morris, *A Wilderness of Error: The Trials of Jeffrey
MacDonald* (New York: Penguin Books, 2012).

9 *McCleskey v. Zant,* 499 U.S. 467, 495 (1991).

10 *United States v. MacDonald,* 641 F.3d 596 (4th Cir. 2011).

11 *United States v. MacDonald,* 32 F. Supp. 608 (E.D.N.C. 2014).

12 *United States v. Morgan* 346 U.S. 502 (1954).

13 *Korematsu v. United States,* 323 U.S. 214 (1944).

14 The DOJ also used the DeWitt report in the Hirabayashi case.

15 Commission on Wartime Relocation and Internment of Civilians, *Personal
Justice Denied,* Report of the Commission (Washington, D.C., December
1982), republished online by the National Archives, https://www.archives.gov/
research/japanese-americans/justice-denied.

16 Arval A. Morris, "Justice, War, and the Japanese-American Evacuation
and Internment," Book Review of *Justice at War: The Story of the Japanese
American Internment Cases* by Peter Irons, in *The Mass Internment of
Japanese Americans and the Quest for Legal Redress,* ed. Charles McClain
(New York: Garland Publishing, 1994), 155–74.

17 Maria L. La Ganga, "A civil rights hero gets his day," *Los Angeles Times,*
January 31, 2011.

18 *Korematsu v. United States,* 584 F.Supp 1406, 16 Fed. R. Evid. Serv. 1231
(N.D.Cal. Apr 19, 1984).

19 Neal Katyal, Acting Solicitor General of the United States, "Confession
of Error: The Solicitor General's Mistakes During the Japanese-American
Internment Cases," U.S Department of Justice, May 20, 2011, https://www.
justice.gov/opa/blog/confession-error-solicitor-generals-mistakes-during-
japanese-american-internment-cases.

20 *Hirabayashi v. United States,* 828 F.2d 591 (1987).

21 The U.S. Court of Appeals for the Ninth Circuit covers the states of Alaska,
Arizona, California, Hawaii, Idaho, Montana, Nevada, Oregon, Washington,
and the territories of Guam and the Northern Mariana Islands.

22 David Wolitz, "The Stigma of Conviction: *Coram Nobis,* Civil Disabilities, and
the Right to Clear One's Name," *BYU Law Review,* vol. 2009, no. 5 (2009):
1277–1329, at 1299.

23 Seth Lipsky, "A Head-Scratching Verdict Against Conrad Black," *Wall Street
Journal,* June 28, 2011.

24 *Black v. United States,* On Writ of Certiorari to the United States Court of
Appeals for the Seventh Circuit, Brief for the Petitioners, July 30, 2009.

25 Conrad Black, *A Matter of Principle* (New York: Encounter Books, 2012), 136.

26 Geraldine Fabrikant, "Lord Black Is Indicted by U.S.," *New York Times,*
November 18, 2005.

27 Tim Arango, "Black Is Sentenced to 6½ Years in Prison," *New York Times,*
December 11, 2007.

28 *Black v. United States,* 561 U.S. 465 (2011).

29 Dealbook, "Judge Sends Conrad Black Back to Prison," *New York Times,* June
24, 2011.

30 Black, *A Matter of Principle,* 308. The feds' strategy of using asset freezes to
disable a defendant's ability to fund a vigorous defense is well known. Robert

Mueller, the special counsel, froze the assets of Donald Trump's former campaign manager Paul Manafort and those of Manafort's children.

31 *United States v. Gonzalez-Lopez*, 548 U.S. 140 (2006) ("Where the right to be assisted by counsel of one's choice is wrongly denied, therefore, it is unnecessary to conduct an ineffectiveness or prejudice inquiry to establish a Sixth Amendment violation.").

32 *Black. v. United States*, Memorandum of law in support of motion to vacate, set aside, or correct sentence pursuant to 28 U.S.C. § 2255 or, in the alternative, for a writ of error coram nobis (June 4, 2012).

33 *Black v. United States*, No. 12 C 4306 (N.D. Ill. 2013), Memorandum Opinion and Order (February 19, 2013), typescript opinion at 7, fn. 2. Judge St. Eve went on to visit effusive praise upon every lawyer who had represented Black through all phases of the case, even going so far as to note "other high profile criminal defendants" represented by some of Black's lawyers, as well as awards and professional recognition they had earned.

34 Powell, *Licensed to Lie*, 277–80.

35 It is unlikely that Congress or the courts will overtly attack AEDPA, though. As the *Harvard Law Review* wryly notes, "Crime is too political of an issue, courts are too concerned about the state of their dockets, and the only people who stand to benefit from more habeas corpus can't vote in most states." Harvard Law Review Association, "Suspended Justice: The Case Against 28 U.S.C. § 2255's Statute of Limitations," 1111.

36 *Harrington v. Richter*, 562 U.S. 86 (2011). For more on the Ninth Circuit's (and former Chief Judge Alex Kozinski's) crusade against AEDPA and prosecutorial misconduct, see Lara Bazelon, "For Shame," *Slate*, April 7, 2016.

37 *Gideon v. Wainwright*, 372 U.S. 335 (1963).

38 See *Murray v. Giarratano*, 492 U.S. 1, 12 (1989); *Pennsylvania v. Finley*, 481 U.S. 551, 555 (1987).

39 Harvard Law Review Association, "Suspended Justice," 1092, 1093.

40 Thomas C. O'Bryant, "The Great Unobtainable Writ: Indigent Pro Se Litigation After the Antiterrorism and Effective Death Penalty Act of 1996," *Harvard Civil Rights–Civil Liberties Law Review*, vol. 41 (2006): 299–337.

41 *Id*. at 309.

INDEX